Confessions
of
An Arms
Peddler

Confessions
of
An Arms
Peddler

DONN R. GRAND PRE

Published by

√chosen books

Lincoln, Virginia 22078

Distributed by Word Books • Waco, Texas 76703

Library of Congress Cataloging in Publication Data

Grand Pre, Donn R
   Confessions of an arms peddler.

    1. Grand Pre, Donn R. 2. Munitions—United
States. 3. Businessmen—United States—Biography.
I. Title.

HD9743.U6G65   382′.45′62340924 [B]   79–12647

ISBN 0–912376–39–2

*To my loving parents, Mae
and Leo, who started it all,
and to my loving wife, Cella,
who continues to fight the
good fight.*

Contents

Foreword   9

Introduction   11

In Goldie's Lair   13

 1 Little Lessons Learned in London   15

 2 The Tadpole   26

 3 The Prairie   37

 4 The Wheeler-Dealers   44

 5 A Little Lesson on Battle Tanks   61

 6 On the Beach   73

 7 The Offer   82

 8 The Second Mortgage   91

 9 Trouble in Arlington   104

10 Crisis in Arlington   117

11 Return to Rome   124

12 Return to Civitavechia   133

13 Requiem for an Arms Peddler   146

14 Showdown   156

15 Troubled Houses   162

16 The Last Big Deal   174

17   Encounter on the Towpath   186
18   The Old Farmhouse   192
Epilogue   197
Author's Note   201

Foreword

OUR COUNTRY WAS founded by men who were prepared to give their lives, their fortunes and their sacred honor to the welfare of the nation.

But something has gone wrong.

The spirit of sacrifice seems to have been replaced by the spirit of greed throughout our land. The results have led many to believe that our nation is desperately sick—perhaps beyond man's ability to heal.

This totally absorbing story—*Confessions of an Arms Peddler*—reveals the temptations the author faced when, after 24 years of faithful and honorable service to his country both in war and in various staff positions in the Pentagon, he was placed in a responsible position of selling arms for the U.S. Department of Defense to foreign nations. He exposes the subtle but persuasive and intriguing tricks professional arms peddlers in the civilian world use to trap honest government representatives and manipulate corrupt foreign officials.

In his own life, when the forces of evil were pressing heavily upon him, Donn Grand Pre discovered an even greater force tugging at him from another direction. Donn found God, the God of his childhood, the God he, like so many of us, had either ignored or rejected in his mature years. Donn turned away from greed with its attendant pains and sorrows and dedicated his life to helping handicapped children find a new life. His entire family is now happily involved in this program.

There is a lesson in this story for all of us, and I think it is this: "If my people, which are called by my name, shall humble themselves,

9

and pray, and seek my face, and turn from their wicked ways; then will I hear from heaven, and will forgive their sin, and will heal their land."

2 Chronicles 7:14

Robt. H. York

Robert H. York*
Lieutenant General
United States Army (Retired)

---

* A West Point graduate, General York at 26 was the youngest regimental commander in World War II, serving as a colonel under General Terry Allen of the "Big Red One" Division. After the war, General York served as commanding general of the 82nd Airborne Division and later was commander of the XVIII Airborne Corps.—THE EDITORS

Introduction

IF JESUS SAID "Blessed are the peacemakers," what does He say about those who sell weapons?

This is what Donn Grand Pre, a veteran arms salesman, had to ask himself. Finding the answer became his own Pilgrim's Progress.

It is also a question that troubles the conscience of millions of Americans.

In 1978 the sale of arms by the United States to other nations soared to thirteen billion dollars. Despite talk of recession it is one market that is continually booming; America expects to sell some fourteen and a half billion in arms in 1979.

"We are providing the means of our own destruction," cry some critics. "Some of our most advanced weapons will get into the hands of our enemies."

The recent fall of the shah of Iran's government might bear this out. The shah's forces purchased twenty-seven billion dollars worth of arms from the United States in the past ten years. Part of this included over 1,500 military aircraft including the F-14, our most advanced fighter, some 1,000 battle tanks and several naval war ships.

Much of this military power could end up in Communist hands.

But many Americans are also worried on a more philosophic level. They feel that too many nations are expending their resources on military equipment instead of developing ways to better feed and house their people. Religious leaders say that selling arms is wrong, that we are violating basic spiritual laws by doing so.

To these critics, government leaders answer: "The financial health of the United States depends on the income from arms sales, otherwise we face an economic depression."

11

Who and what is right?

The question continues to bother millions of thoughtful Americans.

But in 1966 it didn't bother Donn Grand Pre when he commenced a career as an enthusiastic arms peddler for the U.S. Government. What happened to him provides an intimate look inside a multi-billion dollar business.

Donn Grand Pre did finally find the answers to his questions, but not before he went through a crucible of pressure politics, corruption and blackmail, the inevitable sequence of man's lust for wealth, the idolization of the golden calf.

It was a journey that took ten years from 1966 to 1976. In this book he has compressed the events into a two-year period. Within this time squeeze he occasionally uses different items of military hardware or an alternate setting in time or place, either for security reasons or to avoid identifying a specific colleague; for example, the congressional hearings on the main battle tank were held prior to the beginning of his story. As a broker he either assisted or conducted negotiations in seventeen countries. In this story he concentrates primarily on the Italian negotiations as they combine all the ingredients which seem to enter into the sale of military weapons.

For obvious reasons several names have been changed and a few of the characters are composites. Donn states that for the most part, his colleagues were highly respected Washington figures, sincere in their own endeavors, and he has no intention nor desire to malign them, or to malign any individual who made the arms business a personal pursuit. Donn speaks of corruption with a great deal of feeling, both personal and institutional. "I have seen it up close and smelled it up close and fondled it up close," he says. "And when we speak of corruption we must ponder Taylor Caldwell's words in *Captains and the Kings:* 'No man corrupts another; he corrupts only himself and therefore he should not plead for compassion.' "

Donn does not plead for compassion; neither does he pretend to tell the whole story of the international arms business or of personal and institutional corruption.

This is an account how the business of arms peddling affected one man, his family and a few close friends.

DICK SCHNEIDER

In Goldie's Lair

GOLDIE STRUGGLED UP from the recliner and began pacing the floor, obviously upset, emotion flushing his fevered face. "Donn," he groaned, "I'll be 60 years old next month; sixty years come and gone . . . where? They passed so quickly; and I've spent nearly fifty of them making money—always making money. I wanted security, I kept telling myself—a little bit for a rainy day. But, the more I got, the more I wanted; and the more it piled up, the less secure I became."

"My friend . . ." I tried to calm him.

He waved my concern aside.

"Sometimes, I think of all the planes and tanks we sold—all the iron and steel we dropped on Vietnam; bombs dumped on farmers' fields and fragments tearing through thatched huts and burying themselves into the 'enemy'—the bodies of little children."

"Steady, boy," I said. "You're sounding like a peacenik."

He shook his head. "No, I've got to talk it out. Who would understand? My housekeeper? The parish priest of the church I no longer go to? No, I need a true friend, one who's been around the horn. You know war, Donn, you know the arms business. We're friends, but, I've used you, too . . . got a couple of second mortgages out on you in fact."

He laughed shakily and wiped his eyes with a pudgy paw. I shifted in my chair in embarrassment. The tough wheeler-dealer was becoming a maudlin old man.

"You know," he continued, "most of us forget we were once little kids; instead we reject God, sneer at Christ and make a pact with the devil. He comes along and says, 'Fall down and worship me and all this is yours . . . the world and its gold and its power.' "

Goldie stumbled to his feet and pirouetted about the room not unlike a hippopotamus, lifting an imaginary tail in one hand. " 'Here,' the devil tells us, 'just kiss me right here . . . under the tail, just once, and all this is yours.' " He laughed and wiped his nose with a fist. "And then, having kissed the devil's tail—just once—we spend a lifetime kissing other tails . . . for favors, for special treatment, for power. 'But no,' they will tell you, 'not for power but for loyalty. Be loyal to me and all this is yours.' " He looked at me imploringly, "Don't you see it, Donn?"

I nodded and cleared my throat. I saw it, but I really didn't want to see it.

Chapter One

Little Lessons
Learned in London

I HAD BEEN WARNED about him often enough by my colleagues in the Pentagon. "Watch out for Goldie Flynn," they would say. "He can smell a government arms negotiation ten thousand miles away and be there in hours to see what's in it for him."

I knew Goldie Flynn all right. True, I had never had any direct business dealings with him, but he had had dinner at my house several times. My wife liked him, my kids liked him, and I liked him because Goldie knew how to listen to people's problems and could be thoughtful and considerate. Obviously he was a shrewd, pragmatic businessman, this private dealer in military weapons, this former army officer and state department executive who had discovered in his many and varied travels that there was more action and profit on the outside, peddling weapons about the world.

And on that balmy spring evening of 1966 he was in London.

Phil Barrett, the Pentagon's chief arms negotiator, and I were also in London winding up negotiations involving a total package of about one and a half billion Yankee dollars. We were satisfied the way things were going, but the British weren't. Secretary of Defense Robert McNamara had just scrubbed a new missile the U.S. had been developing—an air-to-ground weapon called the "Sky Bolt." To carry it, the British had been designing and building a new bomber. For several reasons, not the least being cost effectiveness, McNamara canceled "Sky Bolt" and the British government was forced to cancel their bomber. Never mind, we said, we'll sell you our new aircraft: two hundred F-4 Phan-

15

tom fighters, fifty of the new swing-wing F-111 fighter bombers, and sixty-six giant Hercules C-130 cargo aircraft.

We ultimately sold all the C-130s, half the F-4s and none of the F-111s.

On that warm spring evening, we were taking time out to relax at an elegant London townhouse where the host, a British industrialist and government arms salesman, was giving a reception. A mixed bag had gathered: military officers, government officials, private industrialists.

And, of course, Goldie Flynn. Even in a crowded room like this, you couldn't miss him.

He moved in my direction, a grin stretched across swarthy features, ivory teeth flashing beneath a bristling, black mustache, a drink held carelessly in one hand. He threw an arm about my shoulders, sloshing a bit of liquid onto my coat. "Oops, sorry, Donn, but no worry; good British gin. It'll evaporate in ten minutes."

He dabbed at the spot with a linen extracted from an inside coat pocket. "Been looking for you," he said. Then, leaning close, he whispered, "We're being watched."

I raised my eyebrows. "CIA?"

"Well, maybe them too," Goldie laughed. "A woman . . . wants to meet you."

I spotted her then, a striking brunette in a red sheath, engaged in animated conversation with my boss, Phil Barrett.

Goldie placed a beefy hand beneath my elbow and propelled me in the direction of Barrett and the woman in red. "Why me?" I asked.

"I just told her what a great guy you are." Goldie smirked. "She can discover the truth later. You'll like Maria. She's different."

As we approached, Barrett turned slightly toward us. "Hello, Donn." Then, turning to the woman, "Miss Valdez, I'd like you to meet my assistant." His arm reached out congenially and wrapped itself about my shoulders, a totally unfamiliar gesture from my mentor who was always cool and reserved. A vague feeling of uneasiness flicked through my mind over the circumstances of this casual meeting, but I didn't dwell on it.

Goldie was right; Maria was different, totally beguiling that evening. There were other differences I didn't discover until later.

Slender with olive complexion she radiated warmth and friendliness.

Maria was nearly as tall as I. Her jet black hair, braided and coiled about her head, and her low-cut floor length sheath gave her a regal quality.

"Miss Valdez, Donn Grand Pre is a very capable negotiator in our chosen field and, I might add, destined for greater things."

The overdone introduction made me feel a bit euphoric. On top of that I was captivated by the flashing smile of Maria Valdez, the luminescent, sparkling eyes and the extended hand—long, cool fingers which grasped mine not too lightly and held on.

"Miss Valdez," I murmured, conscious of a certain awkwardness and almost ridiculously wondering whether my coat was dry, my fly zipped and shoes tied.

"Please," she said, and there was a slight accent, "call me Maria. Goldie has told me so much about you—that you like airplanes and horses, and that your friends call you Donn; so I'd like to call you Donn."

Conscious now that both Barrett and Flynn had faded away, I relaxed. Barrett's presence always made me slightly uncomfortable, as if he were watching for grammatical errors or mistakes in syntax. Barrett liked for his people to have "bella figura" which is Italian for "style."

"I say, Donn, what are you drinking?"

Absently, I gazed at my glass. "Ah, scotch and water."

"But you've hardly touched it."

"Sorry, Maria, I'm a beer man."

"Here, take a sip of mine," she offered. "It may suit you better."

It wasn't that bad, a "marguerita" she called it, and the next time the waiter passed, she ordered two . . . and the next time . . . and the next. The vague suspicion that Maria Valdez might be a pawn of Goldie Flynn's evaporated like the gin on my coat. It had been a long time since a woman had stirred me like this. I was mesmerized, like a high school boy on a date with the most beautiful girl in the class.

By seven, the crowd had thinned out and we were relaxed on one of our host's settees talking airplanes and tennis and horses. I discovered that Maria had many of the qualities of my wife, Ursella: a love of sports and the out-of-doors, except that Ursella never cared for airplanes which had been my first love. Maria held a multiengine rating, I discovered. I found myself fantasizing about the two of us soaring together through the skies. I also learned that her mother lived outside of London with a second husband and that her first, Maria's father, lived in Rome.

"So, you have dual citizenship," I said.

"Not really," she said. "I consider myself Spanish; my name is Spanish and much of my heritage is Spanish. I did attend schools here in England during the early years—what you in America call 'elementary.' That was after the war." She glanced at her watch. *"Madre de dios!"* she gasped. "It's after seven. I'm supposed to meet my mother."

She stood up and I joined her as she walked to the door. A maid brought her a stole which she tossed about her shoulders as Goldie Flynn sauntered up, dark eyes flicking from Maria to me.

"Hey, Donn, Barrett's taking us out for dinner. Maria, will you join us?"

"I wish I could, Goldie." She smiled at him. "I have an appointment with my mother. Another time." She offered me a gloved hand and I took it. "Donn, I've enjoyed this. If you are ever in Rome, we can continue perhaps our tête-à-tête."

"My pleasure, Maria," I said. *"Arrivederci Roma."*

"Arriverderla," she said.

Goldie and I walked with her down the narrow street to a white Jaguar coupe. It was beginning to mist and I held her elbow gently and opened the door. She slid into the plush interior like an otter slipping into a pond. I eased shut the door and she started the car, unwound the window, flicked on the parking lights and waved to us as she swung onto the street. Silently we stood there in the lightly falling rain, watching flickering tail lights fade into the night.

Goldie slapped me on the back. "Soooo, Donn," he boomed, "what do you think of Maria?"

"You're right," I said, "Maria's different." Her leaving so abruptly was a letdown. With a certain pang of conscience I had looked forward to a longer evening with her. I was a happily married man, after all.

My boss, Phil Barrett, had retained a staff car and as the driver sped us from our host's place into the London night traffic, I leaned back onto the upholstery of the front seat, closed my eyes and wondered at the good fortune which had catapulted me at the age of 40 from an ordinary government worker into the world's most select group of weapons salesmen, the international negotiators of our government's department of defense. There were only sixteen of us divided into four teams, but we covered every corner of the earth's surface, meeting with representatives of foreign governments and helping them arrange for the purchase of U.S. battle tanks, jet fighters, artillery cannon, bombs and bullets, rifles and mortars, and all the other marvels of man's technocracy designed to kill other men or destroy their war-making capabilities.

I looked upon it as a very necessary calling. "Power creates peace," Phil Barrett periodically intoned during staff meetings. "Nations evenly matched in arms will negotiate rather than fight." The sixteen of us working for him—and Uncle Sam—had similar charcteristics: we were highly motivated, ambitious, well educated, pragmatic and loyal subjects of our nation's military-industrial complex.

As our staff car threaded through heavy traffic around Hyde Park, I listened to the drone of quiet conversation drifting from Barrett and Flynn in the back seat. On the other side of the rain-streaked window amber street lamps winked in the mist. I was caught up suddenly in memories of my military career which began as an 18-year-old enlisted man in Burma and China during World War II, then as an infantry troop commander in Korea early in 1953 when I had been wounded. That ended a way of life I had come to savor.

It was back home to Dickinson, North Dakota, to a wife and three babies and a job as newspaper editor on a small daily while I completed college in three years. Ursella helped put me through. She was the college nurse. More than once, bone and mind weary after putting the newspaper to bed at midnight, I would rise at seven to attend classes, then go to my wife's small office where I would grab a quick nap on one of the infirmary beds while she outlined a chapter or two for me in a course of history or government. Near graduation, in 1956, a call had come from an old army buddy, Major Dave Chambers. He offered me an opportunity in the Washington office of the army chief of staff. I accepted and worked ten years for the army as a civilian employee in the international arena before moving up to the prestigious office of the secretary of defense.

Those ten years had been a struggle, having to support a family of five children and pay on a heavily mortgaged home in the high-priced Washington area. Now, with sons nearing college, I was in that uncomfortable middle income bracket which blocked the possibility of scholarships yet made tuition bills seem insurmountable.

I pushed the constant concern about money out of my mind and studied the garish lights of Piccadilly as we moved slowly through heavy street traffic and tried to relax. For the past three days there had been constant pressure as we verbally battled the British team at Whitehall during the day, then returned to the American Embassy to grab a sandwich from the little cafeteria before reconvening our team in a small room provided by the ambassador. There we would go over the day's proceedings and prepare for the next, rarely finishing before midnight.

Keeping up with Phil Barrett was tough; in the end I found myself chewing aspirins under stress as he did. As director of foreign military sales Phil eschewed small talk or what he deemed to be trivia. To some he seemed highhanded. A well known senator once blasted him: "Mr. Barrett and his retinue conduct their sales campaigns in an arrogant, obnoxious manner. They freewheel around the world creating hate and discontent wherever they land."

There were times we did just that. When I mentioned the senator's scathing remark to Barrett in his office one day, he shrugged it off.

"If you're gonna make a cake, you've gotta break some eggs. Look Donn," he smiled wryly across the desk toward me, "never forget the name of this game is power and profit. Don't get caught up in the rhetoric of national defense or security. Just remember, the buyer —the foreign ruler—wants to stay in power. To do so, he must have a well trained and obedient military machine. To placate the machine and assure loyalty, he must periodically purchase the latest in equipment for them."

He picked up a silver model of a battle tank on his desk and studied it. "The U.S. has the latest equipment and to provide it, the manufacturer wants to make a profit. We negotiators are merely the catalysts who bring buyer and seller together, cloak them with officialdom, and then fade away when both are satisfied."

He put the tank down. "Noblesse oblige, eh?"

"And remember," he added, "It's the private industrialist and the banker—the entrepreneur with a stake in the game—who really call the shots, not the government bureaucrat.

"To assure success, however, both the buyer and seller need insiders in the government who will jump when their strings are pulled. And between buyer and seller are a thousand outstretched hands wanting a slice of the pie.

"The driving motivation is money—profits and payoff—and in this business, there's plenty of both. Lose the game and you lose the profit. If you're in business and you lose too often, you lose the business. If you're government, you lose the fine office, the wooden wastebaskets and the well-endowed secretary. More than likely you're hustled back to the minors—back to shuffling an increasing stream of minutia-filled papers.

"And also remember," Barrett said, pointing his finger at me for emphasis, "that the gut issues of major arms negotiations are never carried out across a conference table but in the hotels and back rooms of national capitals throughout the world. That means we have to be discreet. Understand?"

Now in the limousine on the rainy London street, I sat up quickly as the driver pulled in front of a popular restaurant. Obviously, this was going to be one of those back rooms and I would have to be discreet. Phil dismissed the driver and we mounted the steps leading to a brightly lit porch crowded with tables and people. Beyond the glassed-in porch was a large dining area. Waiters with white aprons about their middles moved swiftly along the aisles, balancing huge trays laden with linen-covered crockery. The rich aroma of hot roast beef and Yorkshire pudding wafted toward us.

We were escorted by a ruddy-faced headwaiter to a corner of the room. Two tables had been drawn together. A huge man who had been seated at one of them stood as we approached.

Wilbur Baron. After serving two years in the army during World War II he had played tackle for Tulane. There he was known as "Wild Bill," more for his hell-raising than his prowess on the football field. Years of overindulging had expanded his girth, but there was still a lot of muscle underneath the fat. He was still light on his feet, particularly at a conference table, verbally sparring with an antagonist. After college, Baron had been a career officer in the army for several years, followed by a tour in the Central Intelligence Agency. Now as an entrepreneur in the arms business, he had his own firm and was in London looking for private business that might evolve from the government negotiations.

I knew Baron had recently completed a small deal—slightly shady but probably blessed by the CIA and others; he had arranged for a bunch of F-86 jet fighters to be shipped from Canada to Germany where they were laundered so that their origin was lost. From Germany, they passed through Iran and then to Pakistan. At the time, the U.S. government had an embargo on shipments of lethal equipment to India or Pakistan.

We sat down at the table and the waiter took our orders. Soon we began working on the heaping mounds of mashed potatoes, succulent roast beef and steamy Yorkshire pudding over which we ladled a creamy, dark brown, bubbling gravy. Baron speared a slice of beef on his fork and popped it into his mouth. He chewed morosely for a moment, then grimaced and pushed back his chair.

"Hell."

"Whatsa matter, Big Bill?" Goldie asked.

"Meat's too tough to chew," Baron said.

I squirmed inwardly, knowing what was about to happen. The Baron wanted to demonstrate his *savoir-faire.* It was a device he was known for. "Here, I'll trade you," I said. "Mine's as tender as your mother's heart."

"Hell, no, Donn. Then you'd get stuck with a tough piece." He raised a beefy arm in the air and signaled to a waiter. "Hey, over here. My meat's no good."

The ruddy-faced headwaiter hurried over to our table. "Something wrong, Sir?" He smiled nervously at the scowling Baron.

"Meat's too tough," Baron growled.

"Well, now, let's get you another." He laid a hand on Baron's shoulder and gestured to a nearby waiter. "Fritz, would you get this gentleman another order?"

"But certainly. I'm so sorry, Sir." Fritz was bowing low and removing the offending plate. "How do you like the meat, Sir?"

Baron grinned and relaxed. "Well done . . . and hot, *garçon,* hot."

"Yes, sir, and that's the way it will be." Fritz scurried off.

Baron's new order of roast beef appeared and he attacked it with gusto, talking as he chewed lustily. "I'm working a big deal in Italy. Big helicopter purchase. There'll be over a hundred choppers of various sizes to be assembled in Italy on a coproduction arrangement with a

U.S. firm." He turned to Flynn. "The dagos need a bunch of stuff, Goldie: tanks, ammo, boats. Want in on the deal?"

"I'm willing to consider it," Goldie said, as he devoured the Yorkshire pudding. "Italy looks ripe for plucking."

We continued to eat our way through the piles of beef and potatoes. Baron, true to form, had another order while the rest of us went at strawberry shortcake smothered in whipped cream. Baron had two orders of that too. While shoveling in the food, he paused for reflection. "You know I go for seconds on food like Goldie hauls in second mortgages."

There were a few mirthless chuckles. "Second mortgage" was a widely used term both in and out of the government. Translation: blackmail. Many on the Washington scene collected them, finding it beneficial to gather evidence of wrongdoing on the part of their associates. I had heard that Goldie was very proud of his collection, not only as a private arms peddler, but during his years in the state department. As a pragmatist might salt away his insurance policies, Goldie zealously hoarded his second mortgages. Maria Valdez and her beguiling ways flicked through my mind, but I dismissed the possibility. I had my guard up with Flynn.

After Baron and Flynn had departed, Phil Barrett and I sat in the nearly deserted restaurant sharing a pot of tea. He was relaxed that evening, more so than I could ever recall. Phil was a loner back in Washington, married to a socialite who loved parties. Phil would occasionally escort her, but more often she went alone. He was a Harvard graduate and terribly erudite. My colleagues called him a Boston Brahmin and a blue-blooded snob. But, tonight he seemed almost friendly.

"What do you think of our friends and former associates?" he asked.

"Interesting," I replied.

"An understatement, but that's what I'd expect from you." He shifted in the chair and poured the last of the tea from the china pot into his cup. "The British know how to make tea."

"They had to," I said. "Tea kept the Empire together."

He laughed. "Better leave economics to Flynn," he said. "He's the expert."

"Goldie's okay," I said.

"I guess so," Phil agreed reluctantly. "I know you consider him a friend but watch out. Flynn is a friend only so long as he sees it's beneficial to himself. He is dangerous. He once stuck it to one of his friends in the state department; the guy was queer. Anyway, Flynn had photos and mercilessly badgered the guy until he stepped out of a fifth story hotel window."

My boss drained his tea and shifted in his chair. "How would you like an area of your own?" he asked suddenly.

I sat up. "Like what?"

"South Europe. Think you can handle it?"

"Sure," I said, casually sipping the last of my tea in an effort to control my excitement.

"Don't be that sure, Donn," Barrett said softly. He tugged at his foot and draped one leg over the other, loosening the laces of his shoe. "Must be getting old," he mumbled, "feet swell up in the evening."

"Cut down on your salt intake," I suggested.

"Think so?" His look was quizzical.

"Know so," I said. "My dad had the same trouble; doc took him off salt. Two weeks later, no trouble."

"Never again?"

"That's right. You should see him now; he's 70 and still goes pheasant hunting with my brother and me. We've covered every cornfield in North and South Dakota."

"Amazing," Phil said. "I'll try it." He retied the shoelace and stood up, reaching for his hat. I followed him out. Flynn had taken care of the check. We flagged a cab and returned to the Europa Hotel.

Later that night, in the solitude of my eighth floor room, I went over the highlights of the evening. Phil Barrett asking if I wanted to take over South Europe, a territory which included Italy! It should mean a salary increase. Lord, how we could use that!

And then my mind drifted to the lovely and charming Maria Valdez. "If you ever come to Rome," she had said, "we can continue our tête-à-tête." Now it sounded even more intriguing. Running into Goldie Flynn and Wilbur Baron. Coincidence? Uneasily I thought of "second mortgages." Presidents, cabinet members and congressmen had been disgraced by them. One had to be careful.

I stripped and showered and crawled between fresh sheets, clicked on a bedside light and reached for a book on the stand. By mistake

I picked up a Gideon Bible. For a moment I stared at it, remembering my mother and how often she had read it to me as a child. But now it seemed irrelevant and I tossed it aside.

Beside it was a thicker tome, a present from my mother called *A Study of History* by Arnold Toynbee. Knowing of my love of history, she often sent me such books, especially when I was doing graduate work in international affairs at George Washington University.

A quote by Toynbee struck me that night:

> Man achieves civilization as a response to a challenge in a situation of special difficulty which rouses him to a hitherto unprecedented effort. He makes a finer response to adversity and difficult environmental conditions than to "easy" conditions.

I had faced adversity and difficult environmental conditions in two wars, first, in the leech-infested jungles of north Burma, and later in Korea where I led combat patrols night after unending night through stagnant, water-filled rice paddies in the cold and clutching dark. Out of the constant expectation of ambushes from North Korean and Chinese patrols, I had developed a sort of sixth sense—an inner warning system—which enabled me to foretell an ambush, take evasive action or pull back or tighten up a perimeter defense.

Tonight, not once but twice, I received the same sort of signal: at the cocktail party when running into Flynn, and later when we met the Baron. On the surface there was congeniality. Underneath there was a probing, a testing. Okay, I thought, I have been warned; I'll be on guard. Yet I was to learn that even the wily fly can be caught in the glittering gossamer strands of the wilier spider.

Chapter Two

The Tadpole

RETURNING FROM LONDON, Phil Barrett and I shared a taxi from Dulles International Airport. I dropped him at his apartment and continued on to North Arlington and the cul-de-sac on Tazewell Street. As the driver pulled in front of my home, a herd of children descended down the driveway.

"Those all yours?" the driver asked.

"Most of 'em. I won't admit publicly to any more than six."

"Whooeee," he whistled, "lemme give back your tip."

"Oh, no. Those came out of the other guy's pocket. He doesn't have any kids."

"Don't know what he's missin', eh?" He waved and the kids waved and I was inundated by chattering children.

"Hey, Pop, school's out next week!"

"Hi, Daddy, what did you bring me?"

"Hey, Pop, Bruce has a new girl friend."

"Aw, she's not a girl friend, just a friend."

I walked up the sloping driveway to the house, Annette, 5, my brown-eyed blonde cradled in one arm; Colin, 8, clutching the other, and Donnie, my 14-year-old daughter with dark hair and the exquisite alabaster features of her grandmother, leaning against me, arm about my waist. Bruce, 17, and Kevin, 15, two more Nordic blonds grown tall and lean and gangly, tagged behind, each carrying a piece of luggage.

26

"Colin, you've grown an inch. Did you do any fishing while I was gone?"

"Yeah, Dad. Bruce took me and the herring were running, and we caught a million of 'em." Colin, chubby and good natured at eight, was constantly exuberant.

"When are we gonna get a new car, Dad?" Kevin asked.

Before I could answer, Colin jumped up on my back, encircling my neck in a choking grip with a chubby arm. "How do you like that judo hold, Pop? Bruce taught it to me. Can you breathe?"

Tearing him loose with one hand and balancing Annette with the other, I swallowed painfully. "As a matter of fact, I can't. You ruined my pipe."

"Sorry, Pop. I keep forgettin' you're an old guy."

"You better watch it, Colin, or Dad will practice some real judo on you," Kevin warned.

I marveled at our luck every time I came back to the big, brick house in North Arlington. We had bought it in 1963; scraped together a minimum down payment and made an offer on a house that was two years old but looked inside as if it were fifty. A doctor and his wife had it built for a large family: six bedrooms, three baths, a big screened porch on a huge lot of more than thirty thousand square feet. Then their marriage had collapsed, he left and she let the four kids run wild. The house was a mess and most prospective buyers passed it up, but Cella and I saw possibilities. I made a ridiculous offer and the doctor accepted; it hit him the day of the divorce. It took us two years of hard work and a lot of cash to redecorate the place, including repairs to the swimming pool.

I surveyed it now with a critical eye, noting the freshly cut lawn, neatly trimmed hedge, and a new coat of white paint on the garage door. "Looks like your mother has been doing a bit of work about the house."

"I painted the garage doors, Pop."

"Yeah, but I cut the grass."

"Not all of it. Bruce helped you. Hey, there's Mom waiting for us!"

She was. Looking tall and fit and trim from years of tennis, bicycling, skiing and riding. She could really sit a horse. And tennis: I could seldom beat her. She stood at the top of the steps, her brown eyes shining, the baby cradled in one arm. My heart jumped a bit as it always did when I first returned. Here was a woman who liked people, especially children, and she was constantly surrounded by them—ours and others.

And yet, as I stood looking at her, a pang of guilt twinged inside me. There was a growing gulf between us. I couldn't put my finger on the cause, but I had the uneasy feeling that if I looked deeply enough it would be me. I shrugged off the thought and embraced my wife and baby in a bear hug. "Hi, Honey, did you miss me?"

"You know I did," she said, kissing me lightly.

"Cut the mush, Pop," Donnie said. "What did you bring us? Can we unpack your bags?"

Cella was in command. "Kevin and Bruce, bring Daddy's luggage. Donnie, set the table. Annette and Colin, wash for dinner. Donn, take your Tadpole. He's missed his papa."

I took the baby we called Tadpole into the house, the boys dragging the suitcases into the living room. As they tore into the bags for the gifts I brought them, Annette dashed from the room, returning with a gaily colored ball. I sat on the sofa, two-year-old Tad in my arms. Annette slowly rolled the ball across the coffee table. "Here, Tad," she coaxed, "come and get your ball, little Tadpole."

I stood him up where he could grasp the edge. Straddle-legged, head thrown back, eyes transfixed on the ceiling, he watched a spot of light flickering. "Roll the ball to him, Annette."

"Here, Tad, catch it," she implored. He looked down and spotted the slowly moving sphere. He reached both arms for it, moving one tiny foot after the other as he shuffled the length of the table. He gathered up the ball making gurgling sounds of delight.

"Tad can see, Papa! Did you see him watch the ball?"

"Tad isn't blind, Pop. He's got contact lenses."

Startled, I looked sharply at the baby's eyes. "Well, I'll be! You got lenses and they work, eh?" I knelt by the Tadpole as he busily explored the ball with his tongue.

Cella sat down beside us. "Are you surprised that he can see?"

"Yeah," I admitted, feeling emotion. "I am surprised. How much can he see?"

"Well, probably not too much. Colors and shapes right now. Dr. Reynolds says that his vision will improve."

"How long do you leave the contacts in?"

"He's only had them a week, but he wears them three hours in the morning and three in the afternoon."

"How do you get 'em in?"

"It's almost simple once you get used to it, right Doneva?"

Our 14-year-old came over. "It's not so simple for me. Sometimes, I drop them."

"You just open his eyelid, put a little liquid on the tip of a finger so the lens will adhere, and, presto, it's in. He does rub one out occasionally, but we organize a search party and find them, don't we, Colin?"

"Yes, Mama, and I'm the champion finder, right?"

"You are, Darling, you are."

The children crowded close to me. It was a warm welcome home.

I vividly remember the day Thaddeus Daniel came to live with us. It was a hot, humid Wednesday in July 1965, nearly a year before, and it had been a particularly frustrating day at the Pentagon.

I parked in the driveway, sweaty and tired, wishing that I had installed air conditioning in the Ford. Cella met me at the door looking cool, crisp, and kissable in a floral dress and sandals, her wealth of auburn hair piled atop her head. I looked at her, suit coat flung over my shoulder, tie askew. "You're beautiful, Cella—like a tossed salad."

"That's so romantic!" she said doubtfully, then kissed me.

We walked down the hall to the kitchen and I sank wearily on a stool next to the breakfast bar as she slid me a tall, frosted glass of iced tea garnished with mint. I reached for the glass and drained it.

Suddenly, I was conscious of the unusual quiet. "Say, where are the kids?"

"Bruce and Kevin are at Scout camp."

"And the rest?"

"Well, Colin and Annette are eating dinner with the new Canadian couple across the street, and Doneva is babysitting for Vivian Olsen."

"Everyone gone except us. You're up to no good," I said hopefully.

"Well," she said, rubbing my arm, "I do have something to show you."

"You mean something I haven't seen before?"

"Down, boy," she said, laughing. Standing up quickly, she placed her own empty glass on the table and took my hand. "Come on," she whispered.

"I can be had if you play your cards right," I quipped.

"You've been had, buster," she said, opening the door to my study and flicking on the lights.

"What the . . ." My desk had been shoved into a corner of the room and a crib occupied the center.

"Take a look inside."

"A baby! And I didn't even know you were expecting!"

She pulled the sheet back, exposing an infant clad in a too-large diaper and undershirt. He was red and wrinkled, and his legs were curled up as if he were still inside his mother. There was golden fuzz on top of his head and his eyes were tightly shut.

"Isn't he darling?"

"Whose is it and how old is he?"

"Ours and three weeks."

"Cella, you are nuts." I took her by the shoulders and looked into her eyes. "You've gotta stop taking in strays."

"All right, he's not ours; he's just on loan."

"They're lending babies?"

"He came to us through Catholic Charities, product of an unwed girl who died at childbirth. And the baby is blind."

"Holy Mother."

"It's a rubella baby. That's why we have him. Father Cassedy knows I'm an ex-nurse and this one's going to need special care. He may be deaf too."

"But we have five of our own to care for."

"It will only be for a little while—until they can get him into an institution."

"An institution's no place for a kid with his troubles."

"Father Cassedy said he's nonadoptable. Nobody would adopt a deaf-blind baby."

But we did, a few months later, after two eye operations to remove cataracts. I really didn't want the added responsibility, but he had a firm hold on our hearts by then. Even at that, I resented the financial drain he made on our limited resources. Cella said it was part of God's plan. I felt it was Cella's plan and wondered if the day would come when I didn't flinch at window envelopes in the mail.

An hour later the dining room was full of freshly scrubbed kids and the aroma of baked ham and sweet potatoes. There was a brief argument and a short scuffle regarding the chairs to the right and left of Father's. It was settled by the negotiator himself—and a few straws. The shortest and longest won.

It was a delicious dinner, topped off with a bottle of Marques de Murrieta which I had brought back from a previous trip. The chatter was light and meaningless and cheerful. It was seven o'clock in Arlington but midnight in London and I dozed off several times, awakening with a start each time, causing an eruption of snickers and laughter about the table.

"What's the matter, Dad, no siesta today?"

"I was just resting my eyes for a minute."

"Daddy, your head nearly fell in your plate," Donnie giggled. "You look just like Uncle Goldie."

"Daddy, you'd better go to bed."

"No, no, I'll be all right. It's great to be home. I want to hear about school and dates and baseball and broken bikes . . ."

"Hey, I almost forgot," Ursella said. "One of your old friends called while you were in London. He's being transferred from Fort Bragg to the Pentagon later this year."

"Who?"

"Sean O'Malley."

"Who's Sean O'Malley?" Doneva asked.

"He's a priest, an army chaplain; probably a colonel by now. He married your mother and me in the chapel at Fort Benning."

"Maybe Kevin will become a priest," Doneva said.

"No way," Kevin said. "Priests are too serious; they never have any fun."

"Wrong," I said. "O'Malley was always fun to be with—a good soldier and a good chaplain."

"Will you read to us before we go to bed, Daddy?" Annette asked. "How about Pinnochio?"

"Not ol' wooden head again," Colin said. "He read that to us last time he was here."

"But I like it and I can't remember all of it."

"Maybe there will be a new twist in it," I said.

So it came to pass that Pinnochio was read again; from the first wood chip to the last miracle of the Blue Fairy, and everybody was happy that old wooden head finally learned his lesson that deception was wrong and became a real, live boy.

For a moment I was happy too. But a restlessness inside me beckoned: the sinister Lampwick imploring, the Cat and the Fox enticing . . .

The next morning Cella and I were on the tennis court at Glebe Recreation Center. The day was cool and pleasant and I was ready for at least two sets. I figured she'd beat me, considering the shape I was in. She did—for the first two games. Then she seemed to lose her drive and I took the next three.

"Let's take a break," she said. As we walked together to the drinking fountain, I noticed an unusual paleness about her and later, as we sat on one of the wooden benches, her hands were trembling. For a moment I thought she would faint.

"What's wrong?" I asked.

"I'm just tired this morning," she said matter-of-factly.

Something made me pursue it. "Has this happened before?"

"Couple of times. My battery needs recharging."

"Have you been to a doctor?"

"No. I think my body's short of salt." It was a nurse's typical answer.

Cella agreed to see her doctor and we walked the four blocks home. She rested most of the day and I prepared dinner.

Doneva and Kevin did the dishes later while Bruce put the Tadpole to bed and read a story to Annette and Colin. Cella and I sat on the porch, swinging gently on the ancient glider. "Donn, do you have to do all this traveling?" she asked.

"Yes, if we want to keep eating." It wasn't a completely honest answer and we both knew it. I felt that I'd never hit the jackpot with a nine-to-five job. Climbing up that golden ladder was the all-important goal of my life.

She was silent for a long time. Finally she said, "We need you here at home. The kids need you; I need you."

I didn't really believe her, perhaps didn't want to. Cella was always so much in control of things; she was almost domineering and I didn't want to be domineered by anyone. I stirred restlessly, resenting her plea. If Phil Barrett offered me South Europe, I knew I'd jump at it. That would mean even less time at home.

Only the creaking of the porch swing broke the silence as Cella and I sat there. A cool breeze rustled the fringe on the swing cushions. The moment of closeness between us passed. In my concentration on the proposed new opportunity overseas, I forgot about the incident on the tennis court when Cella nearly passed out.

It was later that year, early winter, when Phil Barrett officially offered me South Europe. Now everything I had been struggling for all these years seemed to be in place, waiting for me to show what I could do. The next day Phil called me into his spacious office to discuss strategy along with Colonel Dave Chambers, my old friend from the Korean operation now working in the office of the Joint Chiefs of Staff.

The three of us sat around a coffee table on leather furniture, munching sugar cookies and sipping hot coffee. Phil had set it up as an informal gathering. Dave Chambers helped with his casual attire: sport coat, flannel slacks, loud shirt and an old school tie of Cavalry yellow, dotted with black horseheads.

Dave was of medium height with powerful shoulders and a bull neck. He had been a light-heavyweight boxing champ at West Point and later in Europe. His square, rugged face, and piercing, slate-gray eyes under heavy black brows, set off by a broken nose, gave him a look of ferocity, even cruelty. At heart, he was neither. Although it was Dave Chambers' nature to dominate a situation such as this, he went out of his way to defer to Phil Barrett by slouching in his arm chair, very unmilitary, letting a Gucci loafer dangle from a gaudy yellow sock-clad foot. In contrast, the dapper Phil Barrett sat rather primly in his three-piece Brooks Brothers suit of muted gray and black elastic knee sox.

"The subject of this meeting is Italy," Phil began. "The situation there is complex. The Italian military is stubborn and independent. You know this, Colonel Chambers, and you also know that we deal with their politicians as well as the military for the sale of weapons."

"Just read an article in the *Christian Science Monitor* by Erwin Canham about how you 'merchants of death' are out to control the military wherever possible," Chambers said, reaching for the plate of sugar cookies. "He says we're the biggest exporter of arms the world has ever seen."

I glanced quizzically at Chambers. *Why is he bringing this up?*

Barrett leaned forward in his chair. "True," he said, and there was pride in his remark. "We sell about two billion dollars a year to our allies."

"And quite a sum to the developing nations," Chambers said.

"And why not?" Barrett said. "They have to defend themselves too."

"It's necessary, I guess," Chambers said. "The article indicated that Congress is growing increasingly critical. In some cases we're selling to both sides: Israel and Jordan, India and Pakistan. These poorer nations are using funds for arms that should go into their internal development. Did you know that in Southeast Asia one bullet costs as much as a kilo of rice? That the price of a '105' tank round can feed a family for two years?"

"You can't control how other sovereign nations allocate their resources," Barrett argued.

"Maybe not," Chambers said, "but Canham says you guys are being too aggressive and perhaps even too skillful with these foreign sales."

By now I was getting a little irritated by Chambers' pursuit of the subject. We were here to discuss my new territory, not the philosophical points of arms sales.

Barrett was annoyed, too. "Listen," he said, "without the arms sales our budget would really be in trouble and our balance of payments would be deeply in the red."

"Well, the article raises some interesting questions," Chambers answered easily. "Does the defense department push its sales too aggressively? Does it foist equipment on nations that don't really need them?

Should it be more restrained in dealing with undeveloped nations?"

"Let Congress answer those questions, Colonel," Barrett said. "Our business is to continue to sell, to find new markets and double or even triple that two billion dollars a year. Italy is not a developing nation; it's been a parliamentary democracy for nearly twenty-five years and has enjoyed solid prosperity since World War II. True, they've tumbled thirty governments during that time, but they're our NATO allies and important to us."

He looked sharply at Chambers. "You know all about Italy, Colonel. You were there with the Military Assistance Advisory Group."

"Oh, I do," Dave said. "I know the Italians and like 'em; I'm aware of their strengths and weaknesses."

"Give Donn a rundown of both," Barrett said. "I want him to handle Italy and the other countries of South Europe. More explicitly," he said, looking at me, "I want Donn to manage a battle tank program for the Italian Army."

For almost an hour we discussed the political, economic and military facets of Italy, its drift toward communism, its corrupt leadership, the danger of a military takeover. Barrett then showed us a classified memo from the Italian Minister of Defense to U.S. Defense Secretary McNamara. The gist of it was that the Italians needed new military equipment, particularly tanks. They wanted our help to set up a central base in Italy for the modernization of some ten thousand old M-47 tanks scattered about in a dozen or so European and Mideast countries. These U.S. tanks were obsolete and inadequate without being completely rebuilt. Italian industry could do this for the other countries but not without our help and approval. In return Italy would buy about $200 million worth of armaments from us, including the modern M-60 battle tanks.

"The Italian defense minister wants a representative of the defense department to come to Italy and negotiate the entire program," Barrett continued. "I want Donn to take on that assignment. What I need to know from you, Colonel Chambers, is the plan workable?"

"It's certainly workable," Chambers said, peering up at the ceiling. "The practicality of it is another question."

"In what way?"

"The U.S. Army is committed to support the M-47 for the life of the tank. This is written into every agreement with the countries who have purchased them from us. Some of these countries may object to going to Italy or any other country for spare parts and repairs."

"I believe our colleagues at the state department can convince them of the advantages," Barrett said, studying his nails.

The colonel departed, leaving Phil and me to evaluate the session.

"Good man," Barrett said reflectively, then added, "but I wish he wouldn't get so altruistic about our work."

"He's the best," I said.

"Have you known him long?"

"Since Korea, back in '53. He and a platoon of M-47 tanks saved my life and the lives of my men in the Chor'won sector. We were pinned down by a Chinese force. Dave broke through to rescue us."

"Cultivate those kinds of friends," Barrett said. "Chambers is a comer, a water-walker. He'll soon be a general officer."

I told Barrett I wasn't interested in cultivating anybody. Whatever I accomplished, I wanted it to be on my own merit, not cultivation.

Barrett shot me a cool look. Suspicion there, I thought, or perhaps contempt. Then he shrugged and studied a paper on his desk. I stood, waiting, feeling uncomfortable.

He looked up and smiled again, not unkindly and the tension lines of his face relaxed. "Donn, big things are happening in the Middle East. I'll be devoting more and more of my time to Iran and Israel and the Arab countries. For now, I want you to wind up the current negotiations with Britain and be prepared to go to Italy. Study up on Italy; learn all about the battle tanks, and the other items in the Italian proposal. Keep in touch with Chambers and help him to see the value of setting up this worldwide rebuild program in Italy. Can you handle it?"

"I can handle it," I said, meeting his gaze. Excitement churned within me. I'd show this Boston blueblood how well I could handle it.

He stood up and offered his hand and I took it. "Yes," he said, nodding his head, "I believe you can."

As I left his office, I picked up the last two sugar cookies from the china plate. But it wasn't the cookies that kept me awake much of that night.

Chapter Three

The Prairie

COULD I HANDLE it? As I lay wide awake in bed, hearing the soft breathing of Cella beside me, my mind kept racing over my new assignment.

I knew I could handle the routine of a formal negotiation; it was the nuances that concerned me, the political and financial implications, and men such as the Baron and Flynn hovering about like hungry sharks. Maybe they could be a help; they both knew Italy. Hadn't Phil Barrett tacitly blessed them the night of the dinner in London?

Phil Barrett. He could handle nuances. He had all the élan and polish of the Eastern Establishment, of Harvard and the Brahmins of his native Boston.

Me? I folded my hands behind my head on the pillow. Savoir-faire was one thing I didn't have.

I was the product of the unforgiving Dakota prairie, born in a blizzard, the worst in fifteen years according to my dad, cast into the cold only a few years before the entire economic structure of our country came unglued. For my family and millions of others the crash of 1929 was catastrophic.

My dad had run a bank for a Minneapolis syndicate in Overly, North Dakota. It was a starkly unbeautiful town, implanted in the treeless, endless prairie. Overly had no reason for being except as a coal and watering station for the Soo Line Railroad, a branch out of Minneapolis. Nobody ever intentionally came to Overly. But it was all we had and all we knew. It had one hundred sixty-seven residents including the town drunk, an amiable Norwegian immigrant who subsisted as a handiman, and the town harlot, an amiable, straw-haired, buxom woman who subsisted off the largesse of the locals.

In 1932, when I was seven, my father's bank went broke. We had nothing left but our clothes which we rapidly outgrew, and my mother's jewelry, most of which was sold off during the ensuing years.

Still, we were luckier than most. My grandfather, C. B. Arneson, whom we called Grampa Fatty for obvious reasons, owned eight hundred sixty acres of lush farm land about three miles east of Overly. He was well-to-do until the stock market crash when he lost some money in my dad's bank, but that didn't deter him from inviting us out to the farm when we had to give up our home in Overly.

And there on the farm the days and nights passed slowly. In my sagging bed under the eaves I would lie awake and listen to the driving rain in the summer and the howling winds of winter. I remember sounds: the call of an owl or dog's bark, the crunch of gravel from a passing car, and the piercing whistle of that lonely train clickety-clacking along those two steel tracks that seemed to stretch to eternity. To me, that whistle became a call in the night . . . "follow me . . . follow me."

I grew up on the farm and attended school in Overly. It was a three-mile walk every morning and again at night, except during the really rough weather when my Uncle Carl would bundle my brother, sister and me into a bobsled under a horse blanket on a cushion of straw. Then the matched team of blood bays, snorting and prancing, harness bells jangling, runners swishing over the snow, would carry us to school.

I was content in my early world of farm, relatives and neighbors. I came to know the terrors of the fast-moving, spiraling funnel of a tornado spinning across the prairie, ripping a neighbor's barn into matchsticks; the torrential summer rains with reverberating deafening thunder and eye-searing flashes of lightning; the bliss of wading rain-filled ditches and swimming in a swollen creek; a meadowlark's song of joy after showers; the dazzling white of winter's first snowfall spread across the usually ugly prairie.

And spring came each year with its myriads of crocuses and butter-cups, green meadows and verdant fields. Then, summer's hot sun ar-rived and golden grain and pungent, juicy shoots of alfalfa; and occa-sionally grasshoppers and drought and hail and crop rust.

The "Old Man" as my uncles called him—my Grampa Fatty—
was eternally optimistic. "Next year," he would say, "will be better,
something to look forward to." And we children caught his optimism
and waited for Thanksgiving with its bounty, and Christmas—one
year a gift of a great, colored ball; another, an iron car with wheels
that turned. Life was good and I was happy.

Until I reached 14. Then, I noticed. The Carlsons up the road
had a new car, a nearly new grain truck, two shiny red tractors, a
machine shed to protect immaculate equipment, mowers, seeders,
plows, binders. How white their house, how red their barn, when
compared with weather-seared siding of Grampa Fatty's house.

How did they merit this bounty when we had to do without?

"Donn Rodney, you're covetous," my mother warned.

"No," I said, "I don't want the Carlsons' house or barn or tractor."
But I wanted something just as good and was determined to get it.

So contentment faded and with it, innocence. My world enlarged
and so did my wants. Farm work became drudgery. Sleigh bells lost
their lustre. The prancing bays became plodding, sway-backed broom-
tails. The raging river flowing through the lower meadow became a
sludgy, muddy creek. The farm became confining and I sought escape,
at first in dreams, lying in cool shade on a hot summer day, eyes
drinking in white cumulus drifting on blue sky, the soaring hawk,
wings never moving, dipping, diving.

Then one day there was a drone, like bees, growing ever louder.
Four specks appeared against the azure, growing ever larger: four
airplanes, propellers setting up the most beautiful music I had ever
heard, vibrating, pulsating, reciprocating engines pulling four Boeing
P-12 pursuit planes through the air, flying low over the Dakota fields;
open cockpit army biplanes on their way west.

I yelled in ecstasy, sprang to my feet and ran barefoot across the
fields, leaping like a colt and waving my straw hat. The planes dipped
low, pilots peering down, seeing themselves in me a few short years
before. So they waved and waggled wings and suddenly it was Thanksgiving and Christmas and spring and a meadowlark's song; and something within the boy came loose and soared after the airplanes as
they faded to the west.

Long after the planes dissolved against the horizon, I stood there
staring, eyes wet, lips trembling. Life and adventure had beckoned
briefly and I had responded. Oh, Lord, how long?

Then slowly I turned and trudged back to reality. But from that day on my head was in the clouds. The rickety Case tractor became a multiengine bomber and I and my brave crew were called upon to perform the most deadly of missions. Bridges were bombed and cities and factories demolished.

When I confided these dreams to my sister, Jeanne, she asked about the people living in the cities: the women, the children, the babies, born and yet to be born.

I shrugged and thought about it and shrugged again, the same sort of 14-year-old reaction I reserved for her prediction of the retribution God meted out to sinners in the hereafter. But I changed my technique. The tractor became a fighter and in my daily sorties, I wreaked havoc on the enemy fighters. No women or children here, but men, bold, fearless, willing to die in aerial combat. I became the noble one, goggled and helmeted, leather gloves, and silk scarf streaming, guns chattering, smoke billowing, planes spinning. Daily I shot them down, saluting brave men who had come out second best. No gray areas here; I won them all.

The dreams made dull labor almost palatable; I plowed, disked, raked, and harrowed; I shocked grain, shucked corn, fed hogs, and cleaned stables, spread manure, and cursed the poverty which kept me from driving a convertible like the Carlsons' son.

In midsummer 1941, I was 15 when my sister, Jeanne, came home from nurse's training for a short vacation. One memorable day of her visit had always clung to my mind. I had been on the tractor since dawn and by midmorning it was hot and humid. The air was dead. I pulled on a pair of grease-stained canvas gloves, as the iron steering wheel was hot to the touch. Sweating profusely, I drank often from a canvas water bag suspended from the tool box. By ten o'clock it was warm and bitter and I spat it out, longing for a drink of cold milk from the ice house.

Jeanne must have sensed my need, for her life even then was devoted to service for others. She filled one syrup pail with fresh cookies and another with milk and was waiting for me near a cottonwood grove at the edge of the field I was plowing. As I bore down on the grove, she waved and I swung the old tractor toward the trees.

It was cool in the shade of the cottonwoods. The cookies were oven-warm, the milk cold, and I lay back in the soft grass and leaves, hands beneath my head, looking upward but seeing nothing, half listening to my sister telling me of her plans to join the army as a nurse as she gathered the pails and cups, and scattered the remnants of cookies to the ants.

I rolled over on my belly in the shade of the cottonwoods, enjoying the cool dampness of sparse grass and matted leaves, the dank smell of good earth, feet unfettered from clumsy workshoes, toes burrowing in the humus. I lay there with chin propped by arms, watching the dart-like movements of a big, black, worker ant, first over a dead twig, then along a leaf, halting and moving, conquering obstacles, steadily bearing down on the collection of cookie crumbs.

Other ants were heading in the same direction—the gathering of the clan—all converging on the cookie remnants. I wondered, idly, by what sense were they attracted? Did they smell the choice morsels? How persistent were they?

The thought appealed to me and I blocked the big ant with a hand, forcing it to climb into my palm. There it darted about, dashing to the edge, halting, feeling outward, backing away, moving along a finger, always seeking, never deterred, conquering any obstacle in order to reach its single-minded goal: a cookie crumb.

Peering intently, I flicked him to the ground, watching as the ant moved in on the tidbits. Grasping a speck in its mandibles, it joined the slowly moving stream, each clutching a crumb, moving toward a hidden refuge within their own tiny world.

In my boy's mind came the idea of a test. How much does it take to make an ant give up? I chose the big black one again and flicked him lightly, enough to dislodge the morsel which I placed back with the others. The ant went back, picked out another crumb and began his trek. Again I flipped him and back he went: and again and again. Ten, fifteen times and the ant returned to his task, undeterred by adversity. I tired before the ant, finally rolling onto my back and gazing upward again.

Suddenly, I was conscious of cottonwoods swaying and my ears picked up the gentle sighing of a breeze. The sun was gone, the sky now partially obscured by gathering clouds, white-flecked with gray, but those rapidly were being engulfed by lower, swiftly moving, black masses. Gusts of wind rattled the leaves above me and somewhere a dead limb snapped and clattered through the boughs.

"Storm coming up, fast," Jeanne said.

"Yeah," I said, as I rolled over and stood up. "Can't plow in the rain. Come on, I'll give you a lift back to the house."

As we walked to the tractor, flashes of lightning split the sky and thunder rolled in. A brown cottontail perked up its ears as we approached and darted quickly for the trees. The breeze increased, stirring up a dust devil which moved, twisting and pirouetting along the fence line. As the sky turned ominous, I stooped to uncouple the plow, but the pin was rusty and I scrounged in the toolbox for a sledgehammer as Jeanne hovered near. Two hefty swings drove out the reluctant cotter and the chain-fastened pin clanged against the tow bar.

As I replaced the sledge, the first few drops splattered on the rusted fenders of the tractor. Helping Jeanne to the platform, I flicked the switch, set the throttle and choke, and ran to the front of the tractor. Seating the crank, I spun it.

Nothing.

Rain splatters turned to a steady sprinkle as the wind increased. The lightning grew more severe with rolling thunder steadily louder after each flash, coming in on us like a herd of wild horses. I rested a moment.

"Donn," she called out, "it won't start. Maybe we should run to the house."

"It'll start," I said. Wiping the rain from my eyes, I reseated the crank and twisted again. The engine caught with a roar and I dashed for the throttle and pushed it back and forth several times, then adjusted the spark until the sputtering turned to a steady chugging. Free of the plow, the tractor leaped forward as the sky opened up.

We were drenched in a minute and the rolling boom of the thunder reverberated above and about us as we were caught in the continual zigging, sword-like stabbings of lightning, each seeming to perforate us. I swung the tractor hard to the left, and aimed toward an old haystack which stood starkly against the prairie. Drawing near, I cut the switch, grabbed Jeanne's hand and raced for the protection of the overhang where feeding cattle had shaped the stack into a giant mushroom.

We huddled against the soggy straw, free of the cascading rain, but dazzled by the intensity of the flashes and deafened by percussions.

Jeanne pressed her face to my shoulder and I noticed with some pleasure that I was taller than she. Putting an arm about her, I meant
to be reassuring, but my teeth were chattering and I wasn't sure
whether it was the sudden cold or that I was just scared.

At that instant, a bolt of lightning struck the tractor with a terrible
crackling, sizzling sound. It seemed to explode. It knocked us to the
ground. Jeanne screamed and I wasn't sure whether I joined her.
We sat there, dazed, clutching hands. Then the storm gradually sub-
sided and rolled westward.

As quickly as it came, it was gone, and little puffs of cumulus
rolled in. The sun beamed down and it was bright again. Rain dripped
off the lip of the mushroom and splashed into puddles at our feet.
From the slope behind the hill came the trilling of a meadowlark,
like the melody of a flute after the crash of cymbals and drums.

We took off our shoes, carrying them flung over the shoulder by
the laces as we started walking.

"What about the tractor?" she asked.

"It won't run," I said. "Lightning burned all the wiring; more trouble
and expense for Grampa Fatty."

"Thank God it was only the tractor and not us," Jeanne said. "I
told you He watches over us."

But I didn't heed her. Any message from the Author of thunder
and lightning and meadowlark trills went unnoticed. The example
of the black worker ant stayed: *When you want something, go after
it tenaciously. Dogged, persistent pursuit of the succulent morsel will
win out.*

Chapter Four

The Wheeler-Dealers

TWO OF MY COLLEAGUES warned me about my new assignment. "Italy is loaded with political and financial trouble. At best, it will give you migraines; at worst, it will wreck your career," advised one.

Another said, "Watch it, Donn. Italy is a gathering place for some of the sharpest con artists in the international arms biz. It's where the wheeler-dealers meet to eat, peddle their wares, and give and get their payoffs. Take my advice; stay away from Italy."

All this did was stir my adrenaline. I had played the game enough to know the mine fields. Barrett was always available for counsel. He briefed me periodically through the winter and spring of 1967, then had me assemble a team of experts on battle tanks, ammunition, helicopters, logistics, and self-propelled artillery. We were to be ready to go to Italy in two weeks. A fighter aircraft negotiation for the Swiss which I had been working on was turned over to my deputy so I could concentrate full time on the Italian program.

The following day I worked late in my office and arrived home about 8 P.M. Cella had fed the kids but waited to eat with me. We were interrupted by the telephone. It was Goldie Flynn. As usual, he was ebullient.

"Donn, congratulations! I hear you got a promotion."

"Thanks, Goldie. Bad news travels fast."

"Can you join me tomorrow night at my place for a little business: say about eight-thirty for drinks; maybe dinner at The Embers later?"

A little warning buzzer went off in my brain and a red flag popped up, but I angrily shrugged them away. "Let me check," I said. Hand over the mouthpiece I turned to Cella. "Anything on for tomorrow night?" She shook her head.

"Okay, I'm free."

"Good. Wilbur Baron will be here too. There are things we should talk over before you go to Italy."

"Who said I was going to Italy?"

"That's your new territory, isn't it? Just assumed you'd be going. You can't conduct negotiations by wire—not with the Italians. With them, you gotta get close enough to smell the garlic. See you, Donn."

After placing the telephone receiver in its cradle, I reflected a moment on Goldie Flynn. By his own anatomical description, he had the heart of a lion, the body of an elephant, the mind of a monkey, the appetite of a timber wolf and the courage of a canary.

Which was true only in part. He was big—maybe two hundred pounds—kindhearted to his friends and he possessed a steel-trap analytical mind. He enjoyed eating, but was selective about it. As for courage: well, he did avoid physical confrontation, but he would stand up to any man when it came to his political or economic convictions.

He expressed such convictions succinctly: Vote for the guy who can help you make money. Flynn admitted to a favorite prayer:

O Lord, I don't ask Thee for money.
Just put me where the money is.

There was a bit of pomp and circumstance about Goldie, a bit of the ham, but it had a calculated effect. People usually danced when he whistled and he liked that. To him, people were puppets, easily manipulated.

The next night I drove to the Watergate complex, parked alongside and took the elevator to the seventh floor where Goldie maintained a suite. I thought a moment before ringing the bell. My relationship with Goldie was different now; we were no longer just friends discussing world affairs or the Pittsburgh Steelers. Now I was a government arms negotiator, he a private arms merchant. I was more important to him. I was vulnerable.

Goldie opened the door and broke into a broad smile. He was in stocking feet, and a loosened tie hung limply from an unbuttoned shirt collar.

"Hi there, Donn. Come in!" He slapped me on the shoulder, then led the way across an expensive Esphahan carpet to a padded bar at the far end of the living room. Its top was covered with an array of notebooks and ledgers which he swept into a pile and then dumped in a worn briefcase.

"Been doin' some book work. Here sit down. Grab a stool. What are you drinking?"

"I'll try some of your scotch."

"No sweat." He worked the cork loose from a bottle. "Three glooks do it?"

"And a little soda, if you have any fresh."

"Whatcha mean, fresh? All my mixes are fresh."

"Sure they are at the time you buy 'em. But the fizz goes out when you're gone for a couple months. Why don't you buy six-packs instead of quarts?"

"Quarts are cheaper. Where's your economics?" He slid a drink across the bar. "Have to go up to the kitchen to get ice."

We walked up a spiral staircase to a second level area which contained a formal dining room and a big kitchen. Both were seldom used. We moved to a balcony off the dining room overlooking the Potomac River and the tree-lined Virginia shore on the other side.

"What a view, Flynn. Look at that sunset!"

"Hmm, not bad, but for really fantastic sunsets, you should see them from the beach at Civitavechia."

"Where is that?"

"On the west coast of Italy. I have access to a beach house. I'll show it to you when we're there."

We relaxed in lounge chairs, enjoying the sunset and a delightful breeze.

"Goldie, old friend, you've got everything a man could possibly want, except a wife. Why don't you settle down and take up housekeeping?"

"No slam at you, Donn, but why buy a cow when milk's so cheap?" Flynn laughed and slapped his leg. "You'll see me with a woman in Italy. There's a place for everything in my well-ordered life, and that's the way I'm gonna keep it."

"Have you always been so well-ordered?"

Goldie sighed deeply. "For over thirty years at least," he said. "Longer than that if you count the years I hustled in my old man's junk yard. I was eight when I started in that great smelly place with its high, broad fence, overflowing with wrecked cars, broken bikes, engines and wheels, and pipes of copper and iron and steel. Then there were the hides that made the place stink. But when you're 8, a smelly junk yard is heaven, and you don't mind sorting rabbit skins and skunk hides, or nuts and bolts for maybe a dime a day. When I was older, during the Depression, I really made good dough there when most of the other guys were stealing or doing without. Those two cash registers in my old man's place kept jingling and I kept working: buying, selling, trading, following the old man's advice which was simple enough: 'Buy low, sell high.' "

Goldie laughed at that. "Who needs a course in money and banking. Buy low, sell high," he chuckled, remembering.

"For over thirty years now I've put the old man's ethic to work," he continued, "day and night, in and out of the army. And I've reaped a harvest. But I can't quit. It's a way of life, and there's still a lot of money in the world that's not mine. I guess that's why I never married. No woman would ever put up with me."

"Goldie, be honest. No woman could ever compete with your first love."

"Huh?"

"Money."

Goldie chuckled again. "Well, I found that the international arms business is where you make it. I've wheeled and dealed my way through the Middle East, all across Europe, even dipped into Africa. I peddled surplus German rifles to the Congolese and hand grenades to the Nigerians. I sold French airplanes to the Latinos and British tanks to the Pakistanis. Most of the time, I never even saw the merchandise and worked solely on commission."

He shook his glass, rattling the ice cubes, then closed his eyes and continued. "But, two percent or five percent of a lot of money is a lot of money. It piled up. I tucked most of it away in a bank in Zurich. They take such fastidious care of it that Uncle Sam sees very little of it."

"Okay," I said, "but what about the woman in Italy?"

"Correction," Goldie said, grinning and fanning his moustache with a forefinger. "Women. There's Billie, of course. You'll like her, Donn; she's got a lot of class. Name's Wilhelmina Mason, but we call her Billie. She trusts me to invest her money; she has quite a bit of it. She's also tall, talented and beautiful." He eyed me over the rim of his glass. "There's also Maria . . . you remember Maria Valdez, don't you . . . from London?"

I nodded curtly but sensed my pulse rising. "Oh, yes, I remember Maria Valdez. What's she doing in Rome?"

"Her father lives there. She must have told you. She spends some time with him."

"Give me a little more background on Maria," I said, but the door chimes interrupted my request. It was Wilbur Baron, the beef-eater we'd been with in London.

There was a lot of good natured bantering with the Baron. He was his usual bubbling self which I found wearing after fifteen minutes. Goldie pulled a ham and some cheese from the refrigerator and scrubbed our plans to go to The Embers. I decided to ferret out more details of the tank business in Italy since I was headed there the following week. I knew the position of the U.S. government. Now I wanted to see how it tied in with the private sector. The best defense is a good offense, so I attacked.

"What do you know about rebuilding the old M-47 battle tanks in Italy?" I directed the question at Flynn.

He was sprawled on the sofa, shoeless feet spread out on the carpet, toes twitching in time to soft music from a built-in stereo. There was a hole in his left sock. He was munching on a sandwich and occasionally washed down a bite with scotch and soda. "He's the expert on that one," he said, motioning to Baron with one foot.

"Not an expert," Baron said. "There are no experts in that area. When I was in Italy I noticed their army had a lot of aged M-47 tanks; our ambassador found out they wanted to rebuild 'em while they figured what to do for the long haul—buy our new M-60 tank or the German Leopard. Well, I figured it might be a good deal for someone to set up a worldwide center for rebuilding *all* these old tanks. When I left the government and started my own firm, I decided to try and convince the U.S. Army as well as the Italians it would be good business. They can make some money and we can make some money; that is, if we can get a monopoly in Italy to do it."

"How do we get a monopoly?" I asked. "Must be thirteen countries all over the world with old M-47 tanks."

"You don't without government support," Goldie said. "That's where you come in. It won't work unless there's an umbrella agreement; you know, a covering memorandum blessed by both governments. Then, our government encourages the other countries to come to Italy for all rebuilt and spare parts."

"Those that don't want to rebuild their tanks will sell them cheap to get rid of 'em?"

"Right," said Goldie, "and that's where me and the Baron come in. We buy low, sell high," he grinned.

"You said it, Goldie," chimed in the Baron. "We buy 'em as junk, maybe two-three thousand a tank. Then we ship 'em to Italy. Build up a good stockpile, some for cannibalizing, others for rebuild."

"How about your competition?" I asked. "How about Levy Brothers or Merex Corporation or Shelley, or Mott Haven? They like to buy low and sell high too."

"We cut 'em out of the picture," Goldie snapped. "Part of the purpose of having one government-sponsored program. You guys in the Pentagon set it up as a single, worldwide facility to control the proliferation of armored vehicles. This keeps 'em out of the hands of troublemakers and warmongers."

"Right again, Goldie," Baron mumbled, mouth full of ham. "Uncle sets up an umbrella an' we work under it; keeps the rain off, keeps the money dry." And he chuckled.

Baron took over the conversation: "If we can get our hands on ten thousand tanks, we'll sell every one of 'em. They'll go for seventy-five, even eighty thousand. They'll need new diesel engines and transmissions and fire control systems; cost too much to upgun 'em. Just look at the customers, folks; Jews and Arabs will buy every one we can get ahold of. We'll have to beat 'em away with sticks. What a gold mine. I'm telling you, Goldie, they're standing in the wings, clutching their money like a bunch of Kansas hicks at a boobie show; should be able to get eighty-five to ninety thou apiece." Baron's eyes gleamed, his jowly cheeks quivered, his lips smacked as he kept talking. "The Israelis want tanks so bad they can taste it. We'll give 'em first pick, then we'll sock it to 'em. Boy, will we sock it to those kikes! A hundred and twenty. . . . Sorry, Goldie, didn't realize you were so thin-skinned. No kiddin' though, those guys have the money, or if they don't, their friends in Washington'll see they get it. You know, we'll clear thirty to forty a tank. Goldie, I'm asking you—Goldstein, mine buddy—are we or are we not in clover!"

I stood up and stretched, amazed that the garrulous Baron would parade the monetary factors so openly, even before my team and I had done any negotiating with the Italian government.

"I'll leave the clover for you and Goldie," I said to Baron. "My job is to arrange a tank modernization program for our allies and then to equip them with our newest tanks. Our interest is in the defense of the United States."

Goldie snorted. "Hey, what are you doin', runnin' for public office? You sound like a politician. I don't want to contaminate you with filthy lucre; it's just a commodity I find so very useful. I can wave the flag with the best of 'em, but it don't buy bread or booze or broads!"

The chatter and the drinks went on for another hour, the conversation becoming disjointed and aimless. Goldie made a pot of coffee, mostly to get the Baron on his feet. We drank a cup, said our farewells and I headed for Chain Bridge and North Arlington, rehashing the conversation as I drove. Was I slipping in too deep with these wheeler-dealers? Earlier that day, I had pondered the question, convinced that with the team of experts from the department of the army who would accompany me to Rome, I didn't need the Barons and Flynns. I voiced that opinion to Phil Barrett. He shrugged and dismissed them with the wave of a hand. "They know Italy and they know the deal the Italians want. Talk to them, listen to them; just be discreet."

It was nearly midnight when I pulled into the quiet cul-de-sac on Tazewell Street. I cut the switch of the old Ford and glided into the driveway. There was a porch light on. I mounted the steps and eased open the door, feeling like a teenager sneaking in after a late party. The door to the master bedroom was ajar and I stood there a moment, listening to the gentle, untroubled sleep of my wife. Romantic interludes between Cella and me were becoming more infrequent. She was busy with the children and a group I derisively called "the girl jock-strappers," Arlington women who turned to tennis in the frequent absences of their husbands. Cella was also involved in a program for handicapped kids and directed a "meals-on-wheels" program for the elderly. We had become so immersed in doing our own things that I hardly noticed the barrier rising between us.

Rather than disturb Cella, I decided to sleep in the guest room. Padding down the hall, I passed the nursery, backtracked and went in, leaning over the Tadpole's crib, catching the image of a little guy in the glow of his night light. Curly, golden hair tumbled about a small head resting on a pillow, one chubby fist stuck under a cheek. I listened to the quick and shallow breathing and laid the back of my fingers on his forehead, conscious of Cella's admonition that these rubella babies often get respiratory ailments.

Satisfied, I backed away and went to the spare room at the end of the hallway. Without turning on a light, I stripped and crawled in between sheets smelling faintly of the outdoors. Sheets were made to air, Cella had often stated, and now they enveloped me like a cocoon.

So Maria Valdez would be in Rome. *"Arrivederci Roma,"* we had said in parting the night of the reception in London. I was certainly attracted to her. And why not? She was beautiful, vivacious, charming. Goldie said she was different and she was, in a very appealing sense. Was there danger there? I couldn't recall ever meeting a dangerous woman, but then neither had I ever met a woman I didn't like.

The following Saturday morning Cella and I were sleeping a bit late when there was a knocking on our bedroom door. It was Bruce. "Hey, Pop, a guy from the Ford place just delivered our new car!"

We threw on terry towel robes and followed him down the steps to the driveway. The new car sat there filled with gleeful little Grand Pres—a 1967 Ford Country Squire nine-passenger station wagon. It was cream-colored, with air-conditioning, power steering and russet leather interior. Bruce handed me a packet of material in a plastic envelope. In it was a temporary registration card proclaiming that the car belonged to Ursella and Donn Grand Pre. There was also a sticker on the right window listing the assorted accessories and indicating that it had cost somebody more than four thousand dollars.

A surge of hot anger arose in me against Goldie. Whey did he have to be so blatant? Surely he knew I couldn't accept it. "Golden Heart" Flynn may be displaying his goodness, but I quickly recalled my Uncle Carl's words of long ago: "You never get something for nothing."

How much we needed a new car. The old Ford was decaying and often in the shop for repairs. But how could we afford it? As Cella and the young ones bubbled enthusiastically over every gadget, I mentally did some arithmetic, sighed and joined in the excitement.

I got Flynn on the phone, then went to the car dealer and obtained Flynn's check which I tore up. After some hard bargaining I wrote one of my own for three thousand six hundred. It meant clobbering our budget and I felt a little sheepish in front of the dealer's quizzical look, but I wasn't about to pay the sticker price for a new car. Of course, Goldie didn't care about the price. For him, it would have been an investment—or a lever.

"Just wanted to do something nice for Cella and the kids," Goldie grumbled on the phone.

"Why don't you send her some flowers," I suggested.

The next week, Cella invited him to dinner and for three nights in a row, Blackistone's Florists in Washington delivered flowers: first a dozen long-stemmed roses, then a hanging plant of ivy and finally geraniums in a cast cement planter.

The following Saturday morning I loaded Cella, the kids, and picnic gear into our new wagon and we went for a drive. It was a fun day and we ended it by Little Falls on the banks of the C&O Canal near number seven boat lock. We took our picnic basket across the little foot bridge over the canal and walked along the towpath past the tiny stone house, now white stuccoed with curtains blowing out from open windows—the home of the lock operator. To Colin and Annette, it was the home of Hansel and Gretel.

Not far away was a huge, ancient, gnarled maple tree with a trunk that must have measured three feet through at the base. A vine as thick as my wrist twisted up the trunk to the upper boughs and the end hung free about five feet off the ground. We would boost up a child until he clutched the vine with arms and legs encircling; and then, with a mighty swing, we would propel them up and out and over the placid waters of the canal. There were shouts and screams of pretended fright . . . and always the request for more. And right in the middle of one hearty push it dawned on me: I hadn't thought of Italy for the past several hours.

Nestled against the side of the bank was a fire pit with a huge rock chimney where we built a fire with charcoal and roasted weiners and hamburgers. Chilled potato salad, succulent slices of cold, juicy watermelon, and a huge, green Coleman jug of ice cold lemonade completed our lunch.

By midafternoon we were on our way home where the kids headed for the pool. Shouts of laughter and splashing and the bang-clatter of the diving board echoed throughout the cul-de-sac. Cella and I relaxed on the big screened porch with the Tadpole and a kitten a friend had given him. Tad was rolling over and over on a hemp rug in a circle, the kitten pouncing about him, not quite able to figure out this gleeful, gurgling bit of humanity. Occasionally, she would dart in, dance lightly about on her hind legs and bat softly at the baby's head with muted paws. Tad ignored her and continued to roll.

Suddenly, Cella sprang from the glider. "Good Lord, Donn, I forgot. Father O'Malley called last week and I invited him to have dinner with us tonight. He's due here in a half-hour!"

Sean O'Malley, my chaplain friend during the Korean war. Our friendship had been strained at times on combat locations when he would bum rides with our helicopter pilots, fly to our outposts when we were being shelled by the Chinese and stick his neck into situations where it didn't belong. When I refused to allow him to hold religious services at an outpost for fear the men would bunch up and be too good a target for a shell, he visited the guys in the bunkers and made himself available in my command bunker to hear confessions or to chat in private with any of the men. There was genuine affection and admiration for this gangling priest with the Roman nose, protruding ears and size twelve footwear.

I recall one night when the shelling was unusually heavy and prolonged. It wasn't safe outside the bunkers, much less for him to work his way down the trenches, so he stayed in the command bunker all night long and waited for the Chinese to attack, which they never did. But we had heard their bugles and so we were on full alert. As the night wore on, Sean and I and the first sergeant and the exec began playing poker for small stakes just to pass the time. We grew used to the whistle of incoming rounds and muffled *carrump* until we got a direct hit on our bunker which had twelve layers of sandbags

on the roof. After the dust settled and we relit the candles and our
ears stopped ringing, we stared at Sean. He sat on an ammo box in
the middle of the dirt floor, peering intently at his cards; the rest of
the deck was scattered about the bunker. "Pay up," he said, flourishing
his hand, "straight flush."

This was the guy who was coming to dinner.

Then O'Malley was there and we hugged each other at the door
and did a sort of two-step jig as we skipped about the entryway.

"Donn, you're a sight for these eyes, but you're puttin' on a bit
of weight."

"Weight? You're getting a belly on you like Friar Tuck. And that
sinfully colored shirt—and no collar . . . "

"I came to play not to pray." Looking over my shoulder, he added,
"This must be Bruce." He shook hands with our 17-year-old, eyes
sparkling. I was proud of our oldest, our intellectual. He hadn't yet
caught the fever of the '60s, the rebellion and hostility. He studied
hard and got straight As and wore his yellow hair in a crew cut.

"I kinda' remember you," Bruce responded. "Didn't you visit us
when we lived down by Mount Vernon?"

"Several times. You were just a squirt of a boy. Now, you're taller
than your dad, and better lookin' too."

"Can I get you a drink, Sean?"

"I'm not that thirsty, Donn. I can wait. Where's Cella? Have you
been good to her?"

Ursella came into the entryway where we still stood chatting, and
the rest of the children soon followed, clustering around the big, gray-
haired, crew-cut man of God as if he were a long lost brother. He
was especially fascinated by the Tadpole and carried him back to
the pool where we watched the others swimming. It was Annette
who explained to him, as only a five-year-old can, that the Tadpole
was one of God's special children and He had given him to us to
care for. Later Sean and I moved to the porch where we reminisced
about the wedding—Ursella's and mine—at Fort Benning.

"You know, Donn, I'll never forget the evenin' before the ceremony," Sean chuckled. "When we took you to the club for a last
bachelor blast, you were worried sick. You couldn't eat, much less
drink!"

"I was scared. How come your memory is so good?"

"The pure life I lead. I can recall your tellin' me she was a North Dakota gal, that's all I remember. Did you go to school with her?"

"No. She was a public health nurse in my hometown and worked with the girl friend of my brother, Jim. They introduced us. After we were recalled to active duty, Cella came down to Fort Benning to watch us jump. I remember when Jim made his first jump. He was counting, 'one thousand, two thous . . . ' and the chute popped open. He nearly bit a hole right through his tongue."

Father O'Malley exploded in laughter and I joined him. It was good for friends to laugh together and we enjoyed it. Cella and Kevin came running to the porch.

"Donn—what's so funny?"

We had no answer so I introduced my 15-year-old son to the priest.

"Kevin," said O'Malley, "come here and let me look at you. You've doubled in size since I last saw you, but I remember the dimples and the beguilin' smile."

"Hello, Father. Can I get in on the joke?" Kevin grinned and tossed the thick corn-yellow mane.

"Well, it wasn't really a joke. We were just reminiscing."

Bruce cooked the steaks while we talked. And after we had eaten and nearly everyone else had gone to bed, Sean and Bruce and I lingered by the pool. Bruce, an avid reader and a student of history, was an eager listener while we recalled the combat patrols and night attacks at our outposts by the Chinese and North Koreans.

"I like to hear war stories," Bruce said when I stared at him a bit self-consciously. "Dad never told us any of the gory details."

"There weren't many gory details to tell," I said.

"That's right, Bruce. War is hour after unending hour of boredom, followed by a few minutes of sheer terror, followed by hours of more boredom. What are your plans, Bruce? Are you goin' to follow your father into the service?"

"No way. I don't know what I want, but I know what I don't want."

"You've got the battle half won," Father O'Malley said with a laugh.

"I just don't want to get caught in the mold," my son continued.

"And what mold is that, Bruce?"

"The one that stamps people out for the Establishment."

"I see what you mean! You don't want to be the man in the dark suit carrying the briefcase to work."

"No, I don't. Nor catching the same bus every morning at the same corner to go to the same office day after day, year after year."

Father O'Malley spoke softly, pleasantly. "I admire you for not wanting to be molded into a mechanical man. Don't rush into any profession. Find a purpose in life. Set a goal."

"What's the purpose of life, Father?"

"Each one of us has a different definition. What's yours?"

"I'm confused. The Catechism says, to know, love and serve God, and be happy with Him in Heaven." Bruce reflected a moment. "That's hard for me to understand. Do you know God?"

"I talk to Him a lot . . . and try to hear what He is saying to me. I'd like to know Him better."

"It's easier for you. You're a priest. How do I get to know Him? Or love Him?"

"Do you love your father?"

Bruce was silent for a moment, then cleared his throat. Embarrassed, I suspected. "Yes . . . I guess so."

"As I do mine, Laddy. Well, God is your Father in heaven. He created you and He loves you and He wants the best for you. Can you try and return that love?"

"Yeah, I see what you're driving at."

I listened to the exchange with a mixture of surprise and boredom. Surprise that my teen-age son had an interest in God. Boredom over the vagueness and irrelevance of spiritual talk. Sure, I had sent my kids to parochial school and occasionally went to mass with Cella, but I never had been much for spiritual things even as a boy. I yawned and stretched.

"Donn, we're keeping you up. I'd best be goin'."

"No, no," I said hastily. "Good food and good friends just relax me."

"Thanks for your thoughts, Father," Bruce said as he stood up. "I'm going to hit the rack. Good-night."

Father O'Malley stared thoughtfully after Bruce. "There's a fine boy, Donn."

"He is that, Sean. A bit of a dreamer perhaps, but he'll find himself."

"And the wee one?"

"Thaddeus Daniel?"

"Yes, your Tadpole."

"He'll have a full cup. I'll see to that."

"I'm sure you will, but he'll need special training."

"I've thought of that. We'll send him to Perkins Institute when he's six."

"I've heard of Perkins. It'll be expensive."

"We'll manage."

There was silence for a while, the quiet silence of true friendship. Ours was a bond of camaraderie.

O'Malley broke the silence with the bowl of his pipe, tap, tap, tapping on the arm of his chair, clearing the ash.

"I'll be retiring shortly, Donn. You know, sometimes I have doubts as to whether I fulfilled my role as a priest."

"Never doubt it, Father. You brought a necessary ingredient to all of us."

"I was long on fellowship, short on preachin' the gospel."

"Service men don't want fancy words. You brought the spirit of reason and the purpose of life to all of us."

"I hope so. I doubt that I saved any souls." He was pensive, voice low.

"A man has to save his own soul, Sean. You pointed the way."

O'Malley's face was troubled. "We can't save ourselves, Donn," he said gently. "I have a lot of doubts about things. I may have been better off in a small parish or maybe as a Maryknoller in Latin America."

"You believed in what you told Bruce, didn't you, Father?"

"With all my heart. I only speak what I believe, Donn. You know that."

"Then have no more doubts. Forget the starving people in India. There are people here in Arlington who go to bed hungry at night, hungry for food, for hope, for justice."

"That's true, Donn. But it's not the whole truth."

"You have to be concerned about ole' number one," I continued. "It's a tough world."

O'Malley was silent for a long moment. "Not that tough if you have somebody to share it with—friends, a good wife, the good Lord. How is your marriage, Donn?"

"Not that good, Sean," I admitted, then wished I hadn't.

"Well, I'll put in a good word for you." He stood and stretched. "Time to be gettin' on. Remember, old friend, it takes three to make a marriage."

I didn't answer. What was he talking about? I suspected it had something to do with God and felt annoyance rise in me.

As we walked to his car in the driveway, Sean stopped, turned to me and put his hand on my arm. "Donn, I'd like to ask a favor of you. When the time comes, let me take over the education of the little guy . . . the Tadpole. I've something put by. You'll have enough on your back, gettin' the other five educated."

In the cool of the night, I could feel heat rise within me. "Look, Sean," I retorted as calmly as possible, "Cella and I took him on knowing full well we would take care of him. Why we . . . " I caught myself and sighed. The truth was I had been worrying about the expenses that lay ahead with the Tadpole, but I couldn't let myself admit it.

"Forgive me, Father," I said, and put my arm around him. "Just a little matter of pride, I guess."

Sean took my hand, looked into my eyes for a moment, and then said, "I understand, Donn. Forgive me for being pushy." And then he got into his car and started it. "Watch that pride," he chuckled, leaning out the window. "You know what the Bible says about it."

"Yeah," I muttered, "and I hope you'll be there to pick me up."

The guest room clock struck five and I realized I hadn't slept at all. I went to the kitchen, made coffee and turned on a radio and located an all-night station playing old favorites: Guy Lombardo's "Moonlight and Roses," then a delightful rendition of "Cuddle Up a Little Closer" with strings predominating. I felt poignant, enjoying old memories.

As the strains of "I Can't Give You Anything But Love, Baby" floated off the strings of a violin, I poured a cup of steaming coffee and turned. Cella was standing there in the doorway of the kitchen, curiosity behind a faint smile as she tied the sash about her robe.

"Coffee?" I asked, holding out the cup to her.

"And what's the occasion?" She took the cup from me and sipped slowly.

"It's dance time," I said lightly. "They're playing our music. Listen, that's . . . "

" 'Let Me Call You Sweetheart.' "

"It is, it is; lovely. Hear those violins; that's pissa . . . pissa . . ."

"No vulgarities, please. It's pizzicato; pitz, like prune pitz."

I lifted my coffee cup to her. "It was good to see O'Malley again," I said. "Those were good times on active duty . . . Benning, Rucker, Belvoir . . . and you and I were in love."

She dropped her eyes briefly to hide the hurt. "Are you drunk?" She lifted her head again and looked at me quietly, her emotions under control.

"No, why?"

"You've been wandering all over the house; and now, coffee and music."

"I wasn't all over the house. I was in the . . . "

We were interrupted by a banging and rattling from the nursery. We walked down the hall together, to the baby's room. Thaddeus Daniel was standing in his crib, vigorously shaking it with one hand and banging an empty bottle against the slats.

"Would you say he's hungry?"

"Possibly. He's noisy . . . and spoiled." She turned on the light and instantly, the baby's face reflected the pleasure. He beamed and tossed his head as he gazed at the light fixture.

I came close and waved my hands to get his attention. Although unable to see much without his contacts, he sensed our presence and held out his arms. I plucked him from the crib, and held him for a moment, then put him down on the floor. The Tadpole reached up for a finger, tugging me toward the door and down the hall at a shuffling run. The new game was slide down the stairs and he knew what he wanted. He led me to the door which led down to the recreation room and waited in expectation for me to open it. "Mmm," he said, and then, "mmamaa." He made a gurgling sound and shuffled his feet which meant "open the door."

I pulled it back an inch and the baby stuck his fingers in the crack and swung it open, smiling broadly. He strutted a bit and approached the edge of the stairs, about to do a daring feat. He knelt down and felt for the edge, stood up and turned around a few times. In the meantime, I descended the stairs and waited at the bottom, hoping the little guy wouldn't miscalculate.

He didn't. Instead, he sat down on the top step, twisted about and came sliding down on his belly, laughing all the way. I caught him, but he kicked loose and climbed back up the carpeted steps, stood on the top, turned around and around, laid down, and slid the length of the stairs again . . . and again . . . until Cella called us to breakfast. "Come, children," she said in a gentle tone of love and sarcasm. "Come my little boys; your eggs are ready."

For a moment . . . for just a moment, we did recapture some of the early glow and then it was gone . . . like a flickering candle snuffed by a rising wind.

Chapter Five

A Little Lesson
on Battle Tanks

As MY IMPENDING trip to Italy began to consume my thoughts, I found myself getting more and more irritated over Cella's lackadasical attitude. I returned from a meeting with the army team one night to find her in the master bedroom trying on one of her dresses. I knew her problem. None of them fit as they had only a year before.

Only a few months before, too, she would have met me at the door with a cool drink and a warm kiss. But that had stopped. Was it my demanding job situation or a change of life . . . or faded interest? I puzzled on it for a moment but shrugged it off.

In the midst of my explaining my new overseas assignment for perhaps the third time, she interrupted to ask for help with a zipper up the back and to remind me that we were due at the Chambers' for dinner in half an hour. Chagrined, I zipped her in and walked down the hallway to what we used to call the guest room. It was fast becoming my separate quarters.

Colonel Dave Chambers and his petite blond wife, Kitty, were marvelous entertainers. Two other couples were there. It was an enjoyable evening, yet Cella was quiet the entire time, almost withdrawn, as if her body were detached from her mind.

Driving home, I puzzled about it, but didn't mention anything to her; in fact, neither of us spoke during the drive home from Chevy Chase to Arlington—not a word; not "Wasn't it a great night?" Or, "Wasn't the lobster thermador delicious?" Nothing.

Not even "good-night" as I retired to the guest room where my conscience bothered me and I couldn't decide why. It was Cella who had changed, I felt. I certainly hadn't.

Colonel Chambers called me early the next morning, suggesting a working lunch at the Army-Navy Country Club which is almost adjacent to the Pentagon. "Donn, before we break bread at the club, I'd like you to attend a special hearing about tanks on Capitol Hill."

"Tanks—on the Hill? What committee?"

"House Armed Forces. Two of our generals are testifying."

"That's gonna be my ball game. Count me in."

"I'll pick you up, River Entrance at ten hundred hours."

I strode out of the massive oak doors of the puzzle palace known as the Pentagon at five minutes to the hour. It was a beautiful morning with a light breeze fluttering the huge flags flying from twin poles near the boat dock on the river. A Boeing 727 whistled up the Potomac on climb out from National Airport.

Dave drove up in the old green Porsche, purchased ten years earlier in Germany and treated like a first-born son ever since. As we sped over the Fourteenth Street Bridge and headed up Constitution Avenue toward Capitol Hill, Dave casually brought up the previous night's dinner party.

"What's bugging your frau, ol' buddy?"

"Good question, ol' buddy." I grinned. "What's your verdict?"

"No verdict, just plain nosey." He laughed. "She was so quiet the other night; usually, she's bubbling over. You two had a fight?"

I shifted uncomfortably. "No, not really. It would be a good thing, I guess, if we had. Might clear the air."

"Well, she's sure not her usual self."

"I know. For the last six months, I've noticed a change in her; subtle, but there. Listless, says she's tired a lot. Maybe just bored. Dr. Ryan gave her iron shots and said she was okay. She's putting on weight too, in case you didn't notice. Chaplain, that's about all my troubles!" I laughed. "Punch my card and I'll leave."

"Bless you," he murmured. "You sure that's all—no hanky panky?"

"No hanky panky," I said. "But I may as well admit that along with the other things, our sex life has gone to hell."

"Change of life, maybe?"

"Could be, although a little early. Cella's only 35."

"Look, ol' buddy. Don't let it drift too long. Talk to her, fight with her, but get it out in the open. Kitty and I went through something like it a couple years ago when we were at Fort Hood. I was bucking too hard for a star and she came in second and didn't care for number two. We had quite a spat and I slept in the BOQ for two weeks. Lemme tell you, makin' up was fun, and we've been in sync ever since."

I nodded, saying nothing yet, wondering if it could ever be that way again with Cella.

"Donn, switching subjects, are you gonna be pushing M-60 tank sales in your new position?"

"Not exactly pushing, Dave. Responding to other countries' requests would be more exact. We're *negotiators,* not arms peddlers, remember?"

Dave laughed dryly. "You work for Phil Barrett. That makes you one of the 'Pentagon Drummers.' Barrett likes to sell the merchandise—regardless. My boss is interested in U.S. force readiness. So am I."

"So am I, Dave. Can't we have both?"

"Yes and no. Look at some of those recent arms deals. My boss thinks they're illegal. I agree with him, but we can't do much about it. Neither can you, but as an old army type, I want you to be aware of what's goin' on."

"Okay, what is going on?"

Dave swung the Porsche into the parking lot behind the House wing of the Capitol after getting a wave of recognition from the Hill cop on duty and drove carefully around looking for a parking slot. "I hate to see us peddling our new gear to everyone else and stickin' our troops with worn-out junk."

"Dave, there's no real problem. If the wicket gets sticky—Vietnam or elsewhere—we can gear up production lines and turn out new gear for everybody."

We walked up the steps of the Capitol, and headed for the hearing room. An older congressman with a thatch of gray hair was questioning two generals.

"Two years ago we asked about the operation and maintenance of the army's battle tanks and none of us were too proud of what we had. Now our soldiers are still using those old battle tanks and we're taking the new M-60 tank and selling it to the Italians and the Iranians and the Lord knows who else. Have you any explanation for that?"

The two generals sat upright in their chairs, both appearing calm and very military in green uniforms. The senior general leaned forward. "The tanks going to foreign governments are sales. They're bought with dollars. They are not getting them under grant-in-aid."

"How much less than actual cost are the Italians paying, General?" asked the congressman.

"Well, I believe the agreed price is two hundred thousand dollars. That's total price."

"How much did they cost us?"

"The basic tank is one hundred ninety-two thousand dollars. But with repair parts and delivery, the price would be somewhat over two hundred thousand dollars."

The older congressman nodded grimly. "Considerably over two hundred thousand dollars, General. And isn't the army having to pay the difference out of its budget?"

The general said, "We are taking delivery of these tanks into our inventory. They are then sold out of our inventory."

"I want to know how much the army is subsidizing the Italian government for these tanks."

"Well, our present estimate for a complete tank is about two hundred eighteen thousand dollars."

The congressman twisted slightly to look at one of his colleagues. "Mr. Chairman, my point is very plain. I am not for authorizing or appropriating one dollar in defense funds to subsidize some foreign army." He turned and glowered at the generals, as if they were two truant school boys. "Does Secretary McNamara know about this?"

"Yes, Sir."

"And he has approved it?"

"Yes, Sir, I believe he has."

"Well, I believe we should ask him for an explanation."

The gravel-voiced chairman peered at his gray-haired colleague. "What have you developed, in a nutshell?"

"I have developed the fact that the Iranian and Italian governments are buying our newest tanks through the army at a price below what the army is having to pay for them, and that the army, through the military budget, is subsidizing their military programs."

The chairman boomed. "Let me get this straight: If your statement is true, then our army needs the new M-60s and other armies are getting them before our own. Is this a true statement?"

"Mr. Chairman," the general said, "if I may express the philosophy of this."

"Go ahead."

"The important thing to the army is to keep our tank production line running. To keep it running, we need to sell tanks to some of our allies. Our peacetime army cannot afford to buy all the tanks we must produce to keep a tank production plant in full and economic operation. If we get into a shooting war, where we need to step up production of tanks to say two hundred a month, we can do it very quickly now. But if we let the line get cold, we would have to wait much longer to get it going . . . and at a much greater cost."

Over lunch Dave asked me if I was satisfied with the general's explanation.

"They must know what they're doing," I shrugged.

Dave shook his head. "We get a new tank and you guys are peddling them faster than Chrysler can turn them out. I guess you know President Johnson has given us the nod to modernize Iranian military forces."

"Which means the shah's goatherders and camel drivers are gonna be climbing into cockpits and cubicles."

"Look out, world. Do you really think we can train thirteenth century peasants to fly and maintain modern jets?" Dave asked.

"In a word, no."

"Or to operate and maintain five hundred M-60 tanks?"

"Negative . . . negative."

"So, what's the drill?"

"Oil's the drill, my friend," I said. "The flow of oil, the flow of military hardware: good business."

"Poor tactics."

"Not necessarily; if a balloon goes up in the Persian Gulf, it'll be nice to have some prepositioned hardware close by."

"You mean for our use?"

"You said it, Dave, I didn't."

"Well, five hundred tanks for Iran and one thousand for Italy is gonna use up production for a long time. The chief of staff doesn't care for the idea one bit."

"They're soldiers, Dave. Get an order, continue to march."

"I think it's illegal. Probably even immoral."

"Oh, come on, Dave." I stood up, reaching in my pocket for a tip.

Dave wasn't ready to let the subject go. "Donn, I know your major thrust in Italy is to establish a worldwide tank rebuild program, but are you also pushing further sales of the new M-60 tank?"

"Yes."

"How many and at what price?"

"Well, Mr. District Attorney," I grinned, "that's open to negotiations, but we're shooting for the sale of one thousand new tanks and will probably let them go for the two hundred thousand dollars."

"We're losing money, but we love the business," Dave said.

"Frankly, yes, and we would like very much to beat the Germans and their Leopard tank out of this one. We need to get the M-60 into the inventory of some of our allies."

"If we keep it up with any success, we should be bankrupt by 1970." Dave slapped his hands together. "Maybe the hot shots in the 'E' ring know what they're doing; I sure don't."

I took off for Rome on a Saturday, arriving at the airport about noon on Sunday. As I stepped off the plane, I somehow felt like a gladiator entering the coliseum. This was the beginning of my own moment of truth. A uniformed chauffeur met me at the customs gate. "Signor Fleen sends me to escort you to Cavalerri Hilton Hotel," Benedicto said. The suave Italian sped down the six-lane autostrada, expertly guiding the black Mercedes limousine and chatting incessantly over the intercom. When I checked into the hotel, the concierge informed me that I was already registered and that "everything is taken care of."

I was ushered into a seventh floor suite by an obliging bellhop and escorted about the spacious quarters as if I were a visiting cardinal in to see the Holy Father. The view alone was worth several thousand lire. From the balcony, I overlooked the panorama of Rome, including the dome of Saint Peter's. There were tapestried drapes across a broad expanse of glass; plush carpeting, double beds in one room, and a fancy bath in pink with a matching bidet and a frilly dressing table set against a mirrored wall.

"And this," the worldly little bellhop informed me, "is for mademoiselie."

I wondered who would furnish the mademoiselle.

In an adjoining room, there were white leather chairs and a studio couch facing a built-in television set. Four wrought iron chairs and a matching marble-topped table were arranged at the far end of the room. Beyond the table, hidden by heavy drapes, were sliding glass doors which provided access to a railed balcony where one could look down on a lovely garden and an olympic-sized swimming pool.

There was a covered tray on the marble cocktail table. Beneath the linen was a small ham, a round cheese, several kinds of bread, and a tray of artichokes and cauliflower. Two baskets flanked the ham. Each contained a vintage wine. There was a card on one of the baskets.

"Friend Donn—Looking forward to seeing you again here in Roma. Until that time, please enjoy a small bit of the Baron's hospitality in a not-so-unfriendly country—Yours, Wilbur."

I had just shaved a slice from the ham and popped it between two slices of the dark bread when the phone rang.

"Hello, Grand Pre here."

"Hello, Grand Pre there: Flynn here. How do you like your surroundings?"

"My per diem won't even cover the entryway in this gaudy bit of splendor," I replied.

"Forget about your per diem. Spend it on some presents for Cella and the kids. I know you've got a job to do, and you'll do it your way whether you live in a studio suite or a rat hole off the Via Venetto. So, get off your conscience kick and live a little."

A hot remark was on the tip of my tongue. I took a deep breath. "Okay, I will. In fact, I have a tray of food here that one of your colleagues sent up. Come on over and enjoy some of Baron's hospitality."

"Thanks, I'd like to talk to you before you start negotiations tomorrow. There are some things you should know. You'll also be seeing the American ambassador."

"You seem to have a good insight into my itinerary. What time do I see our ambassador?" My schedule listed a courtesy call at ten-thirty.

"Oh, somewhere around ten tomorrow morning. He's okay—the best thing that happened to the Italians for a long time."

"Yeah," I said. "How about eight tonight."

"About that. Say, I'll have Billie with me . . ."

"Fine, I'll be glad to meet her."

They walked in at the stroke of the hour and although Flynn monopolized the conversation, it was Billie Mason's presence which dominated the room. She had dark hair cut short and feathered; prominent cheekbones and an aristocratic nose; deep, smoked hazel eyes, and a wide, full, sensuous mouth. She was attired in a light green silk dress that clung to shapely legs as she strode about the apartment. There was a charm about her that was chemical, a catlike grace in her walk. While Goldie and I sat on the sofa and talked business, she adjusted the stereo to one of Rome's all night music stations which played mostly American, but also French, German and Italian songs. Occasionally she would hum the melody softly or rise up and offer to fix a round of drinks or pass a tray of goodies from the Baron's offering.

Maria's name came up. Billie seemed surprised that I knew Maria; then she told me about Maria and her life, as if Maria was—or would become—important to me: how Maria was raised by a wealthy aunt and uncle in Madrid when her parents were divorced. Her father here in Rome was a bit of a playboy, a bit of a drunk, but still her father, and Maria loved him; her mother was living in luxury just outside London with her second husband, a horse breeder and horticulturist with money and estate and title.

It was a serious account of affluence. Mentally, I savored this kind of life, and it dawned on me that I had never really tasted the life of wine and roses, of money and position and leisure time to putter with flowers or horses or even to be a bit of a rake. I looked at Goldie sitting across the room. If someone like him could do it, certainly I could do it even better.

Billie talked on and I sank back in the confines of the sofa, enjoying the music and the sound of her voice, which had a husky sexiness about it, whether from sex or too many cigarettes I couldn't tell at the moment. She sat back in an armchair, arms hanging limply along the sides, head tilted back, eyes slightly closed, long legs crossed but very visible. I glanced at Goldie and he was slumped into his great belly, fingers interlaced across it, head forward, gently dozing, oblivious to the music or the sound of Billie's voice.

Finally, she rose up from the chair and stretched, a feline sort of loosening up, and walked to the sofa where she touched the sleeping Flynn's arm and said, "Don't mean to bust up the party, boys, but Donn's had a long flight and needs some sleep. Besides," she added, "I'm tired. Martinis and music make me sleepy."

Goldie trundled to his feet and pulled out a huge stem winder. "Nearly midnight; time sure flies when you're having fun. Well, come on, come on, Billie. See you tomorrow night, Donn. I want to talk ammunition with you."

"Goldie, love," Billie drawled, "better put your shoes on. You may meet somebody you know."

"If they know me, they wouldn't care," Goldie said. He shuffled feet into shoes and I walked with Billie to the door. As they left, Goldie slapped me on the shoulder. "By the way, there's somebody else here you'll want to see. She doesn't know anything about international arms business, but . . ." he shrugged, "I think you have already found her interesting."

"I know," I said, "Billie told me all about Maria while you were sleeping." Goldie's eyebrows arched, but he said nothing.

Billie gave me a gin-scented kiss which was quite pleasant, even though I never had cared for gin.

My team set up headquarters in the office of the Military Assistance Advisory Group (MAAG) the next morning. The Italians were exceptionally friendly, having got the reassuring word from our ambassador that our mission was blessed by Washington. I came to know and like the ambassador; and yet, when it came to matters involving either the buck or the lire, he was ruthlessly pragmatic. He knew what was good for both the United States and Italy. He wanted the new

M-60 tanks in the streets of Rome and he wanted an M-47 tank rebuild facility in La Spezia. And looking long and hard at me, he said that to do so he was willing to support any plan as long as it favored the reigning political party of Italy.

One of my difficult side tasks was to divest myself of the expensive hotel suite without hurting Flynn's feelings. With a degree of diplomacy, I approached the concierge and suggested that since I was rarely in the suite, I could use a less pretentious place . . . "and billed in my name, please." The manager later called back to ask if I kindly would remain in the suite, that there were no single rooms available, but that I would be charged only the single room rate. The Puritan ethic gave way to the practical ethic. Reluctantly, I agreed, wondering if Goldie's orchestration was showing.

As the arms talks droned on over the next few days, I began to see a complex pattern of overlapping bureaus responsible for military purchases and dozens of high, middle and low echelon bureaucrats trying to be important, each claiming he had the ear of the country's Minister of Defense Tostilloti. One problem was trying to keep the military men, government bureaucrats and politicians separated in my mind. They all had an angle or a deal and they all had *bella figura.*

I was told by the military chief of our advisory group that somebody had to sell the minister of defense before there could be any final agreement. "Who would do that?" I asked. The chief shrugged. Perhaps Professor Gulliano or General Garibaldi. One of them would be the bagman. And whichever way the pie was cut a chunk would go into the coffers of the ruling party. There were details he advised me that would "just happen" despite our negotiations. "Leave those details to Flynn or Baron," he advised.

Annoyed, I retorted: "I thought this was *our* party; why the outsiders?" He didn't answer, just looked at me and shrugged.

The days passed. Wednesday was a lengthy day of negotiations at the Italian Ministry of Defense with nothing seemingly accomplished and I returned to the Hilton frustrated, edgy and in need of exercise. At home, I would go for a run or work it off by swimming or tennis. Here in Rome, the pace was so hectic, what with dinners and parties and receptions every other night, and long, drawn-out sessions with my team on the off nights, there was no way to get any real physical exertion. With nerve ends tingling, the only cure was to plunge into the hotel pool for an hour of swimming.

Which is what I did. I swam back and forth across the olympic-sized outdoor pool situated at the rear of the hotel, playing wall tag: back and forth, back and forth, the only occupant; even the lifeguard was gone. I was interrupted by the bell captain who informed me that a call was holding. I took it at the poolside office.

It was Goldie. The Baron was having a party for us at a place called the Coq D'or. His girl friend, Isabel, was in from Madrid, and she was a friend of Maria's . . . "Maria Valdez. You remember her from London, eh? Gorgeous . . . both of them."

Flynn picked me up an hour later in the same Mercedes limousine with the same chauffeur who had met me at the airport. We drove to the southeastern part of the city to a lovely ancient mansion built by an eccentric in the 1920s who had modeled the place after the Sistine Chapel. There were gaudy paintings of chubby angels and bearded saints on the ceilings, and alabaster statuary throughout the house which was now an upper class restaurant. The mansion was situated in four acres of parklike shrubbery and walkways, with dining areas inside and out.

We met the others inside the Coq D'or and it was the beginning of a strange relationship that continued for many months: sometimes intimate, occasionally bitter, always intriguing. There was Billie Mason, who I had found was good company, and the Baron with his voracious appetite and garrulous dialogue, and his Spanish girl friend, Isabel, several years younger and only several pounds lighter than the Baron.

And there was Maria Valdez. I had been deeply attracted to her from the moment she had held out her hand at that first greeting in London. She was beautiful, but she was more. There was something electric about Maria. I likened this second encounter to the challenge and excitement of becoming acquainted with a complex airplane or an unmanageable horse.

I don't really recall the witty chatter that took place that evening; at least, it seemed witty. We sat together in a small room with subdued lighting about a fireplace that had a low fire burning; then were ushered upstairs through a huge dining room to a private alcove.

I don't recall conversing with the others either. I know that Maria was captivating during the first course of cold slices of red salmon with white wine, and became more so as the evening progressed. Later, seated in the same room downstairs with the fireplace grown cold, I stirred up enough internal fire to suggest she join me for dinner the next night at Piccolo Mundo. Ah, she was so sorry, but the night was already reserved for her father. But, perhaps, she suggested, if I were remaining in Rome for the weekend, I would accompany them to the beach at Civitavechia.

And then, it was there, but ever so briefly: the warning flag, a faint alert, the signal of a pending ambush that probed at a Calvinist conscience. But something else was there: a certain chemical substance heightened by flickering candlelight, attracting, dimming the Calvinist conscience. And, as the others droned on, voices muted, I studied Maria's features in the half-light, shadows accentuating slightly famished hollows beneath rather prominent cheekbones, the finely chiseled nose of alabaster, the rather full and pleasing mouth, the startling cat green eyes under shadowed eyelids.

"Time to break up this bash." It was Goldie struggling up, smothering a yawn. It was a cue and we all stood and said our farewells there in the room with the candlelight flickering. I took Maria's long, tapered fingers in my own and held them lightly as she peered into me with those startling cat green eyes. "Until Civitavechia," she said.

"Until Civitavechia," I said huskily.

Chapter Six

On the Beach

I AWARDED MY TEAM a long weekend for all the days and nights we had been working until well after midnight. Then I left for the beach shortly after noon on Friday with Goldie, Baron, Isabel, Billie and Maria.

The beach house at Civitavechia, a two-hour drive from Rome, was an architectural monstrosity with huge, rambling, high-ceilinged rooms, and a yellow stucco exterior. Yet for all its expansiveness, there were only two baths in the place, both identical and located upstairs at the end of a long hallway.

To avoid any embarrassment, Goldie modestly marked each of the baths. On the door of one, he tacked a pair of his red polka dot shorts; and on the other a floral bit of diaphanous nylon, obviously the property of Billie Mason.

There were seven bedrooms along the hallway and when we arrived about 6 P.M. on Friday, Goldie, in the assignment of rooms, placed me directly across the hall from Maria.

I threw my luggage on the bedroom floor, changed into swim gear and raced for the beach. It was perfect for a swim that early summer evening in 1967. Maria, Billie and Isabel joined me, but Goldie and the Baron preferred a less vigorous tonic. Rolling up their trousers, removing socks and shoes, the two fat friends strolled along the sandy beach, drinking beer and talking.

The four of us ran through the surf and swam out to an anchored platform. I was winded when I reached the raft after swimming against the breakers. After crawling onto its rough surface I collapsed, watching the three women approach. A week of tension slowly drained away and an inexplicable feeling of euphoria washed over me. Maria was first to reach the platform and I hauled her aboard. Laughing, she flicked off a white cap and shook loose her jet black hair. Billie was next and I gave her a hand up. Isabel was last and it took both Billie and me to get her onto the raft. There was a lot of Isabel and she was not in as good physical condition as the other two.

We all sprawled on the raft and watched an orange fireball sink into the Mediterranean Sea.

It was Billie who suggested a race back. "Just give us a ten second start, Donn." I took it as a compliment.

I stood on the rolling raft and watched as they dove in—the tall, lithe Billie Mason in a yellow bikini; Isabel in a one-piece white tank suit which accentuated her ample voluptuousness; and Maria, slimmer than the other two but perfectly proportioned and wearing a frilly floral suit of several shades of lavender.

Later, while the girls dressed for dinner, Flynn and the Baron took me on a tour of the cottage. I met the middle-aged couple who were preparing the meal and who lived year round on the property which was jointly owned by Flynn, Billie Mason, the U.S. ambassador, and a general of the Italian Army. The property included a cabin cruiser. It also included a wine cellar and sauna bath.

"It's not a real cellar," Goldie said. "We couldn't dig down very far because of the high water table, but it keeps the wine colder than warm."

There were fifty or sixty bottles pigeonholed along one wall and Baron, the connoisseur of the grape, selected two for the dinner.

We were on a huge screened porch facing the sea. Cool wine, flickering candlelight, amiable talk, hot food and the sound of gently lapping waves against the shore made it a beautiful evening. After dinner Isabel suggested a rubber of bridge. When I begged off, Goldie suggested that Maria show me the cruiser. As Billie searched for cards, Maria and I headed for the pier. There were five boats at anchor.

"Come, Donn," she said, tugging at my hand. "Help me to the deck. I will start the engine while you untie the moor line." She stepped down to the gleaming deck as I held her hand. The boat was a thirty-two-foot Chris Craft, white with blue trim.

"You mean we're going out?"

"But of course," she laughed. "What else is there to do with a boat? Unless you would rather not," she added.

"I think it's a great idea! Let's go." Maria was wearing white sneakers and flowing white bell-bottom slacks with matching blouse. She scrambled along the deck and disappeared into the open-top cockpit. As I worked loose the line, I heard her fumbling about, then caught the flicker of amber cockpit lights and soon the low rumble of a marine engine.

"All right, Donn, cast off the line!"

I threw the rope to the deck and leaped after it. As I slid into the cockpit alongside, she backed out the boat and swung the prow to sea. Expertly she guided the craft around the blue channel markers for about a half mile, then slowly added power as we headed into open water. I shared the captain's seat with her as she pointed out various landmarks. A million stars glittered above in a black sky. Our wake caught their reflection and flicked them about like fireflies. She placed my hands on the wheel and stood up beside me, dark hair streaming in the breeze, face tilted, sheer beauty in the dim glow of the amber lights. One hand rested lightly on my shoulder.

A little later, she reached down and cut the throttle. I swung the wheel to face the distant lights of Civitavechia and we drifted, small waves slapping against the hull, the muffled "gluga gluga" of the underwater exhaust the only sounds. I stood up beside her, steadying myself with one hand on the windshield, conscious of the gently rocking boat, the faint, tantalizing aroma of expensive perfume, and the exquisite softness of the woman leaning against me, strands of silken hair occasionally blowing across my face. I breathed deeply of the moist, salty, night air, touched with lilacs, and slowly exhaled.

"As close to heaven as I'll ever get, Maria."

"You believe in heaven, Donn?"

"Why, yes, I guess I do."

"And hell?"

"I guess so," I nodded, slightly puzzled. "I guess each of us makes our own hell . . . or heaven."

"And you believe in God, too?"

"Yeah . . . yeah, I do." I tried to inject a degree of solemnity in my answer; and yet the mind doesn't always cooperate. For some reason, I thought of an old joke of the hot-blooded young man taking his very religious girl friend for a country ride where he parked, hoping for a little cooperation. She wanted to talk about the hereafter. Finally, in exasperation, he exploded, "Honey, if you ain't here after what I'm here after, you'll be here after I'm gone!"

It wasn't that funny, but laughter welled up within me and the more I tried to restrain it, the funnier it became until a chuckle became a giggle which turned into a full-fledged belly laugh. I collapsed weakly on the pilot chair.

"So, you laugh at me." There was hurt in her voice; yet, I could not contain myself. I giggled like a school boy.

Holding up a hand, I denied it but couldn't explain. I shook my head. "Gosh no, Maria," I gasped. "I . . . I just remembered something funny . . . so long ago . . . long ago . . ."

"Well," she demanded, hands on hips, feet planted firmly, wide apart, "tell me so I can have a laugh, too."

The humor faded and I reached for her hand. I tried to explain the story, but it lost something in the telling. I bombed.

"I don't understand," she said. "I don't get the funny."

I patted her hand. "It really wasn't that funny, Maria. I was just letting off a safety valve."

"I don't understand."

"What I mean is . . . I've been uptight all week; you know, too much pressure. Now, with you, I relax, and . . . it just felt good to laugh."

"Ahhh," she said. "Now I understand!"

"You do?"

"But, yes. This fellow, he thought maybe he could make love to the girl and she wanted to only talk about God and heaven . . . and you thought maybe it was you and me, eh? Yes, it is funny!" And she laughed and for a while I thought she was laughing at me, but it was real mirth and infectious, and I joined in again until I was sure Goldie and the rest of our crowd could hear us in the beach house three miles away.

She leaned against me as we giggled and I kissed her and her lips were warm and full and she lay nestled against me. I wanted very much to capture that moment and hold onto it; the dark hair blowing loosely in the night breeze, the warmth and softness of a cheek against mine. Did I believe in heaven? Sure. We were there . . . now . . . together. It was utterly still for a small part of eternity save for the gentle rock of the boat and the lapping waves and muffled engine. We neither moved nor spoke, but at that moment, somewhere in the Tyrrhenian Sea off the beach at Civitavechia, we established a bond of intimacy that transcended both friendship and sex. Oftentimes, over the next hectic weeks and months, my mind would flick back to that small bit of eternity, trying desperately to recapture that mood, that moment.

But she stirred and moved away from me and wordlessly I eased forward the throttle, turned the boat about and headed for the channel markers. She scrambled, catlike, onto the deck, out on the prow and stood there straddle-legged, bell bottoms billowing, long hair streaming. And still later, she returned as we approached the channel markers and she took over and expertly ran down the channel to the pier where she maneuvered alongside. Rope in hand, I jumped to the dock and snubbed it as she cut the engine and joined me on the pier.

She was unusually quiet as we walked hand-in-hand back to the darkened beach house. I sensed a certain tension when we walked up the wooden steps leading to a screened porch and she withdrew her hand. I held the door for her and we walked through the porch and into a hallway where a dim light glowed. Suddenly she turned about and faced me in the hallway, hands again on hips. "So?" she said . . . or "so!" A question or an exclamation? I wasn't sure, but there was a certain amount of static electricity in the air and suddenly I was uncomfortable.

"So . . ." I said; "a lovely evening, Maria. Good-night, *Hasta Manana.*" I held out a hand and she took it in both of hers and some of the tenseness dissolved. In the half-light I caught the shadows of her smile and a glow in the cat-green eyes, as if a candle behind them had been lit. "I'm going for a run along the beach," I said.

"Go with God," she said, releasing my hand. *"Hasta manana."* I watched as she turned and walked swiftly, quietly, quickly to the end of the hallway and up the flight of stairs. I turned and retraced my steps to the beach where I kicked off my tennis shoes and jogged slowly along the shoreline, breathing deeply of the cool, moisture-laden, night air; unfettered, free as a bird, enjoying the quiet serenity of a star-speckled sky, hearing only the waves breaking gently on the shore and the "squinch, squinch, squinch" of my feet compressing the wet sand. For a moment, even my mission to Rome was almost forgotten.

I ran nearly a mile, turned for no special reason and jogged back, stopping to retrieve my shoes. I walked along to the cottage, tiptoed quietly upstairs where I took a cold shower in the antique bath, dried with a coarse towel and eased down the long, narrow hallway to my room.

It was Maria who suggested a picnic. While the others lay in the sun on the beach that Saturday morning, Maria and I were in the kitchen. Juanita packed a wicker basket with her culinary delights as Maria bantered with her in Italian. There was enough food for six, but Juanita added a cluster of grapes and a cool bottle of red wine. I carried the basket to the Mercedes while Maria changed into white slacks, a silk blouse, and a bright green scarf about her throat.

We drove north along the coastline, past the road which angled off to the town, and then turned east on a little-used dirt road which brought us into a rural area of olive groves. Maria indicated a side road, little more than a trail, and I nosed the Mercedes up a rocky incline.

And then, we were there: a cluster of poplars on the far side of the hill. It was cool in the shade of the *chopos,* as Maria called the trees, and there was a gurgling spring close by and a small stream.

"This is my private oasis," she said, as we walked about the area and waded barefoot in the stream. "I don't know if anybody else is aware of this paradise."

We walked together hand-in-hand back to the cooling shade of the poplars to the spot where we had left the basket. Maria flipped out the blanket covering the basket and spread it at the base of a gnarled tree. I sat on the blanket and reclined against the tree as she knelt to sort out salad, sandwiches, plates, forks. I cradled my head in my hands, leaned back, closed my eyes and listened to the gentle sighing of a breeze stirring the poplar leaves. I heard the muted wind in the trees and the sound of a bird and the faint clatter of a picnic being laid out and the soft humming of Maria. And I was transported back to a day in the fields on the old Dakota farm, back to that day my sister, Jeanne, brought cookies to me as I was plowing.

We had sat in a grove of cottonwoods eating and talking; Jeanne, who later became an army nurse, then married and was still helping people as a head nurse at St. Luke's Hospital in Fargo, North Dakota. I wondered if Jeanne remembered the black worker ant I had watched as we ate cookies and how tenaciously he had pursued the crumbs. How persistent he had been! And I wondered if I had been as tenacious, as persistent, in my pursuit . . .

"Donn, wake up." It was Maria calling. I had dozed against the tree. I sat up, startled and saw it was Maria, not my sister; but the dream was so real, as if that day of the storm had happened last week instead of twenty-five years ago. *Time,* I thought, *the great healer and the great thief.*

As we nibbled the food Juanita had prepared and sipped the wine, we talked nonsense. At first we sat apart from one another, the basket between us. Then I moved next to her and put my arm around her shoulder. There was warmth and tenderness and electric tension. I drew her close to me and felt my throat tighten. "Maria . . ." It was a husky whisper.

She stiffened. What had been a soft, pliant, willing, woman, was suddenly a protesting frightened girl.

"No, Donn, please, no!" It was an urgent whisper.

"Maria!" My voice was hoarse, strained. "What's the matter?" I glanced at her and the fear belonging to a cornered animal was in her eyes. It shocked me back to reality. I stood up and lifted her to her feet.

"Maria, I'm sorry; I really am; I'm sorry as hell."

"Donn, I don't know, I don't know!" she sobbed, choking, shaking her head in anguish. I clutched her shoulders and tried to force her eyes to mine, but she kept her head down like a child and tried to press her face against my chest, crying in great body-wracking sobs which tore my heart out.

Finally, she was still in my arms.

"Donn, I thought this spot, this day, a cool bottle of wine . . . and you . . . would banish my inhibitions. I wanted to . . ." She stopped and the tears came again. I smoothed the ebony hair and patted her on the shoulder.

In the Mercedes she sat, subdued, next to me all the way back to the cottage.

It was Billie—after a vigorous swim and candlelight dinner—who cornered me later that night. "Well, how was it, Sport?" she asked and I played dumb.

"How was what?"

She laughed the husky, throaty laugh. "You know, the love feast . . . the picnic . . . Maria."

I patted her arm. "Great, it was great, perfect weather, ideal spot, beautiful . . ."

Billie arched the plucked brows, a knowing smirk on her face.

The next morning was Sunday. I went downstairs before eight. The caretaker couple sat rather stiffly at the kitchen table drinking coffee. The husband, Tony, was dressed in an ancient black suit, white shirt and gaudy, striped tie, while his wife, Juanita, wore a starched dress, purple straw hat with a sprig of artificial flowers and, under her hand, a prayer book.

The proper *"bon journos"* were exchanged and I said, "You're going to mass."

"Si," Tony said. "We go churcha . . . Sunday."

"You like *cafe?"* Juanita asked.

I held up a hand. *"Si,* Mama, I get it."

While I was pouring, Maria walked in, dressed in a two-piece lightweight suit, carrying white gloves and purse, a white lace mantilla over her hair.

"Bon journo, Maria," I said. "Coffee?"

"Bon journo, Donn. Tony . . . Juanita. Yes, please." She hesitated, then came near and stood by me as I poured a second cup.

"You're going to join us for mass?" I asked.

She looked up at me, a quizzical look on her face. "You're going to mass?"

"Why not?" I said. "It's Sunday."

"Yes, it is . . . it is," she agreed.

We took our coffee to the table and sat there, Maria making small talk in Italian. Finally, Tony pulled out a huge watch.

"We go," he said.

We went—in the limousine, Maria and I in front, Tony, with his wife, sitting in back and looking like the mayor of Milano.

I hadn't been to a Catholic mass in a long time, but I enjoyed it.

Maybe it was Maria—or her presence—as she was totally engrossed in the mass which was still conducted in Latin at that time.

"Mea culpa, mea culpa, mea maxima culpa," murmured the congregation, and as Maria beat her breast, I joined in.

The great and sincere religious devotion of the entire group fascinated me, particularly during the offering of bread and wine and the holy communion. The entire congregation virtually rose as one and formed lines, shuffling to the front of the church to receive the body of Christ, except Maria and me. Maria read her prayer book and I sat beside her. Tony and Juanita returned, hands clasped, eyes closed, save for a peek now and then to find our pew.

After mass I took them to a restaurant in the main part of the business district. There was canteloupe and ham and croissants and jam and coffee. Maria was subdued but spoke often to Juanita and Tony or responded to their questions or interpreted for me.

Juanita spoke to her and looked at me and smiled, then held a work-worn hand to her face.

"What does Juanita say, Maria?"

"She says . . . that we are a lovely couple." She looked at me and there were tears in her eyes. She swallowed involuntarily and I touched the back of her hand gently.

"Grazie," I said to Juanita who giggled. Then to Maria, I said, "Tell her that in us she only sees the reflection of her long and happy life with Tony."

Maria spoke rapidly and then looked back at me, her eyes still filled with tears. She fumbled in her purse for a tissue, then stood up and walked rapidly toward the entrance. Juanita appeared startled, then struggled to her feet and limped after Maria.

"Salud, Tony," I said lifting my cup.

"Salud, Señor," he replied, raising his; then, shaking his head, "Women!"

Chapter Seven

The Offer

THE WEEK FOLLOWING Civitavechia was a whirl of activity involving meetings day and night at the U.S. Embassy, the office of the U.S. Military Assistance Advisory Group, and at Italy's ministry of defense. The evenings found me coaching my team in the hotel suite for the next day's planning. I drove them as hard as Phil Barrett used to drive us in London, for the success of this Italian negotiation had become a burning goal within me. However, there was a difference between my team and Phil's; the team here in Rome had more *esprit de corps.* We worked hard, but there was always time for a night out or a sight-seeing tour. Even when working late, we surrounded ourselves with good food and good wine.

One evening, we prepared a document which, when typed the next day at the embassy, became the vehicle whereby Italy was to be handed the worldwide rights to rebuild, repair and maintain all of the M-47 tanks in thirteen countries, including spare parts supply. "Vot a deal!" Williamson, our tank expert, exclaimed. Inwardly I was excited. If we pulled off this one even Barrett would have to congratulate me.

The draft document served as a basis for a series of meetings with the U.S. ambassador and his staff, the MAAG chief and his military people, and with representatives of the Italian Ministry of Defense, as well as with select members of U.S. and Italian private industry which included both Flynn and Baron.

Individual members of the team broke loose later in the week and headed north to look into Italian manufacturing capabilities and to determine what support would be needed from the U.S. Army and U.S. industry. I became even more optimistic.

And then one morning I met with two Italian generals. Something was apparently wrong and it wasn't their lack of knowledge of the English language. They knew that I was trying to arrange for an adequate stockpile of spare parts; in fact, twenty million dollars' worth. But they were balking over seemingly insignificant points. The chief of the army section of the U.S. military group was with me and I finally realized, after a few nudges with his foot, that we were wasting our breath. We broke off the meeting and the U.S. colonel advised me that negotiations over the table would move no further until certain under-the-table transactions took place. "Fine," I explained, "but that isn't my department." I left, feeling frustrated, and headed for Francisco's to have lunch with Goldie Flynn. As we sat at the small table hunched over heaping plates of spaghetti, I voiced my annoyance at the impasse.

"The answer is obvious," Goldie said.

"It is? To whom?"

"To me, the Italians, to any arms dealer, including your boss." He smiled knowingly and popped the now-laden fork into his mouth.

"Except me, the negotiator."

"You're still new at the game; you'll catch on."

I grunted and speared into the delicate pasta.

"Time for a little 'baksheesh'; time for the laying of the green," Goldie nodded sagely.

"Payoffs," I muttered.

He nodded. "You get the picture. Only we don't use those words; too crude. Not exactly payoffs, but certain people and certain political parties have to be reimbursed. After all, it takes a lot of time and effort, and arranging, if you will, to make any deal go."

"Who does this arranging?"

"Not you, certainly; you're government. No, this is our category— us private dealers . . . U.S. and Italian . . . anybody standing to make a few bucks. Time for us to discreetly move some funds from our pockets to their pockets."

"Who moves the money from your pockets to their pockets?"

"Well, in the small-time shenanigans of American party politics they're called 'bagmen.' In our trade, we call 'em 'orchestrators' or arrangers or agents. They're important links because they know where the money has to go for a deal to move."

"Who's the orchestrator here?"

"For our purposes—and your program—he's a Professor Nicholas Gulliano."

"A professor, eh? What does he profess?"

"Just about anything." Goldie laughed. "You'll have to meet the professor. He's 'a nice a guy.' You'll like him."

"The Professor; is that a gangland moniker like The Enforcer or Machine Gun Kelly?"

"No, he actually was a professor a few years back." Goldie twirled a wine glass by the stem. "Professor of political science at the University of Milano, I believe. It seems he pursued academics, coeds and the grape with equal fervor and was considered highly competent in all three. But, some of the charisma faded after he was discovered in bed with a young student *and* the older wife of a faculty member; *ménage á trois,* I believe the French call it." Goldie chuckled and drank the dregs of the wine. "Ah! Those French! Well, so ended the professorial pursuits of our Nick Gulliano. He left Milano with only the title and a ballpoint pen and drifted here to Rome where, through a series of connections, he ended up on the unofficial payroll of the minister of defense. Of course, it helped to have General Saragati, a bit of a rake himself, as his brother-in-law. Ahhhh, connections!"

"How much money?" I asked.

"Never ask how much as a first question: first, to whom? The 'how much' is always negotiable."

"You have to start somewhere."

"Try the ruling political party; they have the power; it's their machine; and it's up to us, including our kind and benevolent Uncle Sugar, to make sure the wheels are greased."

"How much grease does it take to keep the party solvent?"

"Hmmmmm, maybe ten, maybe even twenty million dollars; plus a few for the boys along the way."

Recalling the words of the Baron in Goldie's Watergate apartment some months before, I said "I'll leave the payoffs to you wheelers and dealers. I'll stay away."

Goldie held up a hand. "No, you can't. You're government, therefore official. Your presence at a dinner where the financial arrangements are discussed is important."

Suddenly the smell of backroom intrigue got too strong for me. "Count me out," I said. "The secretary of defense would have both cheeks of my butt hanging from the twin flag poles at the Pentagon."

"No!" Goldie exploded. Squiggling his chair closer to me, he took a deep breath, slowly exhaled, the garlic in his breath almost overcoming me. "Now look, Donn," he said, almost fatherly, "you and I have known each other for a long time. We're different, which ain't necessarily bad. Lemme tell you that on this deal, there's a lot more at stake then whether I sell a little ammo or whether Chrysler sells a few tanks. There's a relationship at stake."

"Yeah," I said, "the one between me and my job."

"Listen, my friend," he said, sitting forward in his chair, "Let me acquaint you with a few facts of life. It's your job to see the deal goes. The relationship is between governments—the Italians and ours. I'm talking about stability and anti-communism. We gotta maintain a center coalition government here at all costs or this country will go to the commies. It's either that or another Mussolini."

"And you're telling me that my little negotiation will be the deciding factor?"

"Yes," he said, "that's one of the deciding factors."

I thought for a moment, suddenly realizing that I wanted this transaction to succeed just as much as Goldie.

"Okay," I said, "what do I do?"

Goldie visibly relaxed, sinking back in his chair. "Nothing . . . except come to dinner, be polite, hoist a few with the boys, eat hearty, nod occasionally and just be sociable. Be yourself." He laughed and struggled to his feet. "I don't care what they say, Donn; you're okay." He slapped me on the shoulder. "One of these days, I'm gonna make you an offer you can't refuse."

As we strolled out I felt somewhat annoyed, as if Goldie had taken a part of me. "Look," I said, trying to collect myself, "make me an offer; only make it plain and make it direct. I don't like surprises."

"Donn!" he said, eyes opened wide in a mockery of a man in shock.

The sun was down, my team members had gone back to the states, and I was left to sit in on Italian-style negotiations. These were held across a table in the massive dining room of our host for the evening, one of the money changers, a vice president of the Banca Unione

Finanzaria. The only thing we negotiated—at least while I was there—was a seven-course meal with two kinds of wine.

There were fifteen of us around the table, all male, mostly Italian, save for myself, Flynn, our ambassador, and a representative from General Precision.

And Goldie was right. All I had to do was drink, eat, talk, socialize, and occasionally nod my head. I was aware of one startling fact, however. Never once was the formal government-to-government negotiation mentioned, nor was there a word about money in any form. My head was nodding of its own accord by midnight and I was grateful to Flynn when he volunteered to drop me at the Cavalerri Hilton. Nick Gulliano, the professor, joined us in the Mercedes. As we sped through the light traffic, Gulliano laid an arm about my shoulder.

"You are remarkable fellow, Donn; do you mind if I call you that? Our gooda friend, Goldie, calls you Donn, which is a shortened version of Donaldo, eh?"

"No, just Donn . . . two n's."

"Ah, *bona,* Donn it is, and I am Nick. Nick and Donn; we should be gooda friends."

"Right," Goldie interjected.

"You college man, Donn?"

"Yeah, George Washington University."

"Ah, I know that university ina Washington, in you capital city. I visit you campus onea time . . . "

"Hey, your memory's real good, Nick."

"Sure! I'm a college man too. I like a sportsa too. I likea soccer."

"Great game, Nick."

"You havea children?"

"Yes, six."

"Ah, *bona, bona;* you must be Italian!"

"So is the Pope," I said.

"*Bona, bona,* Goldie, you hear that? So isa the Pope!"

"Donn is a real card," Goldie said.

"Hey, Donn, what a you likea—boats, acars?"

"Planes are my weakness, Nick. I like cars too."

"You havea you own airplane?"

"No, I belong to a flying club in Washington. Owning a plane is beyond my means."

"No, Donn, if you likea somet'ing, you getta: airplane, boat, car
. . . women . . . "

"Ambition. That's what made our country so great," Goldie said.
"You want something, you go after it."

"Whata airplane you likea?"

"I guess, if I had the cash, I'd buy a Beech Bonanza."

"Goldie, you know such airplane?" Gulliano asked.

"Nope. I only know wings, tail, propeller. Donn's the aviation expert."

"How mucha cost this Beecha Banana?"

"Oh, a good used Bonanza runs twenty-five, thirty thousand dollars."

"Used? Who wantsa used?"

"Well, a new one's outa sight; probably seventy-five thousand."

"That's nota so much."

"Too much for my diet."

"A college man likea you . . . a smarta man . . . seventy-five thousand, one hundred thousand dollars isa not'ing."

Nick removed his arm from my shoulders and turned formal. "Signor Grand Pre, you havea some give in you final price on M-60 tank?"

"Give, Nick?"

"*Si*, give. You tell General Saragati final price is two hundred thousand no?"

"That's right. You probably know those tanks are costing my government two hundred fifty thousand dollars."

"*Si*, I know. I no understand how come you cuta pricea so much,
and say final. Why you have no more give?"

"How much more give are you talking about, Nick?"

"I'ma talka peanuts."

"Nick, I thought you were a professor, not a peanut farmer."

"Peanut farmer. That's a *bona!* Hey, Goldie, you hear that?"

"Clever," Goldie said.

"I talka five thousand dollars a tank, Donn. Donn, you tell General
Saragati tomorrow meeting, you final pricea one hundred ninety-five
thousand."

I didn't say anything and for a moment only the hum of the limousine
tires on the pavement filled the car.

Goldie turned around in his seat and said, "Sleep on it."

"Yeah, I will," I muttered, then turned to the professor. "Look, Nick, let me . . . sleep on it. I'll have to cable Washington."

We drove under the canopy at the Cavalerri Hilton and Goldie stepped out. I shook hands with the professor and followed Flynn out of the car. He held out a beefy hand.

"Have a good night, Donn," Goldie said, preparing to step back into the car.

"You and Nick going partying?" I asked.

"No, we're going back to Santini's. We didn't have dessert."

"We didn't?"

"No, there's a big pie being sliced and I want my share."

"Well, old friend, don't get meringue on your fingers. And . . . " I found it hard to get the words out, "tell our buddy, Nick, I'll think about the Beecha Banana."

I had a restless night, pondering the power structure both in Rome and in Washington, D.C. I never really understood either power or its application. Oh, I was aware of Aristotle's equation: *Knowledge equals wealth equals power.* And I was aware of the extension of that equation by one of my political science professors: *Knowledge equals wealth equals power equals corruption.* And I had been around enough to know that fundamentally that's how the system works. Machiavelli's Prince knew it and Metternich knew it and I imagined that LBJ and McNamara and Ho Chi Minh knew it too. There was another equation bandied about Washington at that time. "Power equals peace," the idea being that if a country or group of countries had sufficient weaponry available, other countries would not attack and there would be a state of affairs, rather nebulous, called peace.

I was for peace . . . who isn't? But, I was also for military preparedness. I knew how naked we were in the 1930s and at the beginning of World War II. I liked my present role in government—relished it in fact—helping countries to keep militarily strong, a common defense against the enemy. But, who was the enemy? I wondered. Monolithic communism? Was this what was creeping into Italy, growing stronger every year, not only in Italy but in Portugal and France and other European countries? How could we stop its spread? By intrigue, by pouring funds clandestinely into corrupt governments, in collusion with corrupt political machines? Fight evil with evil?

But, what the hell, I told myself, *the commies do the same, only in a much more insidious way.* They charm and beguile a people by promises, by allowing them to hope for something better; but, of course, communism had proven time and again it was not better, it was worse; it was a repressive dictatorship of the left, as bad or worse than a Mussolini or a Hitler.

And, of course, I agreed with Flynn that unless we could contain the spread of communism in Italy under a democratic form of government, another Mussolini would arise, would take over the military and with it, wield another form of absolute power.

Well, what's the answer? I had no answer, except the eternal verities, perhaps, to which nobody but the Christians paid much attention. Unable to go back to sleep, I picked up the Gideon Bible on the bedside table and flipped through it, but the *thees* and *thous* and *thys* and the begetting and the begatting told me nothing. I set it aside and thought about a "Beecha Banana" and new station wagons and college educations for all my kids and a decent chance for the Tadpole. In this world money was the answer; with it, you could be your own man and do your own thing. Without it, you were a pawn on a loaded chess board, subject to the whims and fancies of others. Goldie had said, not once but many times, "Every man has his price." What was mine? I was beginning to believe I had one; only the amount was in question.

I cabled Barrett at the Pentagon, strongly urging that we cut the M-60 price and the answer was back in two hours: two hundred thousand dollars was it. There was an "eyes only" statement at the end; "There is enough heat from Capitol Hill at $200,000. Good luck."

I spent most of the day in the embassy composing a lengthy message to Barrett outlining the progress of negotiations. Shortly after I had fired off the cable to Washington, I received a call from Flynn.

"No give on the two hundred thousand dollars," he stated calmly.

"Right. Barrett said there was too much heat from Congress already."

Goldie was silent for a moment. "Drop by my suite about six o'clock, Donn. I've gotta go out of town."

"Okay, Goldie. How was the pie?"

"Pie?"

"Yeah, you were slicing one last night."

"Oh . . . pie, pie. It was cherry pie, Donn." He chuckled. "Goin' on a fish fry next."

"Watch for bones, Goldie. One day, one of 'em's gonna stick in your throat."

"This cat knows how to eat fish, boy. See you at six."

Click.

Chapter Eight

The Second Mortgage

I LEFT THE EMBASSY at four-thirty and walked three blocks up the boulevard to catch a little blue shuttle bus to the hotel. It was spring in Rome and all the shopkeepers along the Via Venetto were digging up the boulevards and planting rainbows of luxuriant flowers. One day the streets were bare, and the next, they burst forth in a wild paroxysm of color. The mood of spring was in the air and it was reflected in the promenaders strolling along the famous way.

Goldie's door was ajar and I strode through the richly carpeted living room into a bedroom. Clad in candy-striped shorts, he was seated on the edge of a king-sized bed with a telephone squeezed in the hollow of his mammoth shoulder. He was talking to a contact in Bonn, Germany—something about lawn mowers and spare parts and availability and shipping arrangements. It was inconclusive and Flynn was agitated. As he listened, which wasn't very often, he poured salted peanuts into his mouth or sipped from a drink.

"Well, do the best you can, Andy, and call me first thing in the morning. We've got to get the dope for Baron." He banged the receiver into its cradle and stood up, draining the glass.

"What's up, Goldie?"

"Trying to keep the deal from coming unglued. Wilbur flew over to Madrid to work on the Spanish. I'm trying to get the surplus tanks out of Germany for the consortium." He walked over to a closet, selected a pair of pants, and, like a hippopotamus doing a ballet, pulled them on. Glancing at me, he grinned. "A leg at a time, Donn, just like everybody else. How'd your day go?"

"I don't know, Goldie. I'm worried about the negotiations," I said. "However, I'm getting some interest again from the Italians. We polished up the agreement, shot a message back to Barrett, and told them I'd be back in Washington this weekend."

"I'm heading back there myself next week after I work out an ammo deal as a part of the package." Goldie also represented an Italian firm that was eager to sell ammunition to the United States, some twenty million dollars' worth.

I walked over to the stereo and flipped a button, turned the dial to Rome's station which specialized in classical music and sank back on a davenport. "Do you think you can convince our government to buy ammo from the Italians, Goldie?"

Goldie, who was now shaving, stuck his head out of the bathroom. "Why not?" he said. "You expect the Italians to buy a lot of stuff from Uncle, you gotta buy something in return. Why not ammo?"

"Guess you're right. There isn't much else we can buy here until the tank rebuild plant goes up; only the official position of the guys in Defense before I left was that there is no requirement anymore for offshore procurement of ammo."

"That's for public consumption," he said, coming out of the bathroom as he toweled his face. "The boys are still smarting from that bad publicity when we had to buy back those five hundred and seven hundred fifty pound bombs we sold the British. Remember when we were so low on those? Paid the British four times what we sold 'em for just to buy 'em back." He grinned and patted his chest. "I made some money on *that* deal."

"And I expect you're going to make some on this one too."

"Sure. That's the name of the game. I think we can convince the Secretary we'll be forced to buy quantities of high density ammo from foreign sources over the next five years, so why not from Italy?"

"What's your cut on a deal like that, Goldie?"

"Who, me? I just work for the fun of it." He patted some cologne on his jowels.

"Do you clear five percent?"

"No, that's a little high for ammo; more like three percent."

"Let's see; that's about six hundred thousand dollars on a twenty million dollar sale, eh?"

"Close enough. Why? Are you interested?"

"Interest is relative," I said.

"I could use your help convincing the Pentagon to buy twenty million dollars in ammo from my company here for the grant-in-aid countries," Goldie continued.

"I'll talk to the logistics people when I get back."

"Do that." He struggled into a shirt. "You've got a wonderful wife, Donn." He nodded thoughtfully: "A nice little wife and a bunch of charming kids."

I nodded, silent.

"Gotta think ahead, Donn. Kids'll be going to college soon. You and Cella will want to retire some day."

"We'll hack it."

"I could use you in the business next year," Goldie said. He sat down in a chair across from me.

"Don't tempt me: conflict of interest." I tried to laugh.

"You're in conflict of interest right now, drinkin' my booze."

"Booze is not conflict, it's a gratuity."

"Lemme give you some gratuitous advice," he said, his voice lowering. "I'm moving into the Israeli market soon. It's really growing, and they are moving into territories we can't touch from the United States. It's gonna take all my time for awhile; I'll need somebody to take over Europe. Consider it."

I shifted uneasily in my chair. "There are a lot smarter guys than me, Goldie, who know your business better than I do. What about Smitherson in Bonn, or Bray right here in Rome?"

"No. They won't cut it. I need a man who can keep his mouth shut; a man who isn't afraid to take a chance—after you make sure the stakes are in your favor."

"What makes you so sure I'm your man?"

"Several things. We've known each other for nearly three years. We're cut different, Donn, but, in this kind of business, that's not a bad arrangement. We're complementary. You are what I'm not. Don't get me wrong; I'm not apologizing for being like I am. I took a lot of time and a lot of money to produce this . . . ." he patted his belly, "and this . . . " touching a finger to his forehead. "Up 'til now, with the backing I had in Washington, I could swing most any deal by myself and a select group of operatives here in Europe. But I'm plunging into new ventures too good to let slip and I need help."

"I'll think about it."

"Do it—seriously. I've got excellent backing, people I want you to meet. In this business, Donn, you need 'angels,' protectors, guys who will cover for you, lobby for you. You also need financial backers, silent partners, who like the color green and don't want to get mixed up in the arms business. The same color attracts the inside men— those in the Pentagon or the White House or State who will feed you the right kind of dope at the right time. I've got 'em. I've got me a team."

"Goldie," I said slowly, "give me a straight answer." I caught his glance as he looked up quickly, and held his gaze. "Do you . . . have you ever had any doubts about what you're doing?"

"Doubts?" His look, unblinking, was quizzical, as if he didn't under-stand the question.

"Well, yes," I said. "You're always so sure . . . never doubting that your course of action is the only one. You steamroll people. I have a hunch you would use and discard people—even your friends— when they no longer suit your purpose. Tell me, Flynn, did you ever have a mother?"

That hurt him and I saw his face sag and he looked away and cleared his throat and jiggled the remains of his drink. Slowly, he placed his glass alongside mine and sat down heavily on the edge of the bed.

"Oh, I had a mother," he said, massaging swarthy cheeks with the ham-like hands. "Mama . . . we called her Mama . . . and there was Papa too." His voice faded and he cleared his throat again. "But let me tell you about a certain night . . . too many years ago . . . the night of the crowning. Maybe that'll answer your question about doubts." He glanced at me and the sparkle was gone from his eyes and I leaned against the bureau wishing I hadn't asked the question.

"My crown of thorns is still here." Goldie circled his pate with a pudgy forefinger. "But I've worn it well over the years. The night of my crowning took place in Kansas City, done by a cluster of clean-cut, grade school boys. That particular day, little Mauri Goldstein— me, Donn—had showed them up in composition class. A show-off, 'a smart alec kike,' they called me. I went to work after school at the old man's junk yard, floating on a cloud of teacher's praise. I was the only boy in the class who produced a satisfactory composition on 'What My Country Means to Me.' Sure, Mama helped some with the structure, but the ideas were mine and the expressions and the emphasis as I read it to the class, they were mine; I believed in what I had written. And I say it unashamedly—I loved my country. And the 'excellent' across the top of the first page and the teacher's fine words and little Molly Saunder's smile of admiration—they were mine and they were glory."

"No better praise," I said, sitting on the edge of the bed.

"My classmates, or a portion of 'em—Calvin Ridge and George Tucker and Bill Burke and Chester Welles—didn't hand in a composition. In 1932 there were better things to do during an evening than write a composition; they pilfered cigarettes and stole Cokes from the old Syrian's delicatessen; they told dirty jokes and ogled women and shot pool. And I can hear them shouting that evening as they closed in on me, moving down the darkened street like a pack of hounds after a rabbit. 'Hey, George, you know what my country means to Fritz Mueller?' 'Yeah, Chet, it means my country 'tis of me, sweet land of Germany, my name is Fritz . . . give me some sauerkraut, don't let the juice run out . . . give mee-he-heee a bottle of beeeeerrrrr and I'll stay here . . . ' " Goldie croaked out the song and chuckled ruefully and rubbed his cheeks.

I laughed, remembering the song.

"They were waiting for me that night, Donn. I always left the junk yard at nine and walked the seven blocks home. Papa stayed behind to do the books. They waylaid me three blocks from the yard. I can see them swaggering about and calling 'Hey, Mauri, was a beautiful composition . . . ' 'Yeah, Mauri, who wrote it for you, Mauri?' 'Did you ever swipe anything, Mauri?' 'Hey, he never swiped nothin'. ' 'Come off it, Goldstein, you're a kike, ain't ya? All kikes swipe.' 'Did you see Molly Saunders grin at the Jew boy?' 'Hey, Jew boy, did ya ever get any of that?' 'Nah, he couldn't; Jew boys have the ends of their wee-wees snipped off, right, Mauri?' 'Hey, let's have a look. Come on, Goldstein, drop yer pants, we wanta look at your wee-wee.' "

Goldie held his hands to his face, moving the fingers slowly over his eyes and down his cheeks, probably feeling again the embarrassment and rage and fright of that night, every detail carved forever into the reaches of his mind.

"Then, the pack closed in and I lashed out and got in a couple good punches and then went down in a melee of swinging arms and kicking legs and cursing mouths. They punched and kicked and poked, but they got in each other's way and their hassling attracted a cop. His whistle scared 'em off in four directions. As for me . . . a few minor aches, tender ribs, a sore behind, and a bloody nose. But," and he paused and bit his lip and shook his head . . . remembering . . . "inside I was emotionally crucified. I bent, choking and trembling, to pick up seven sheets of crumpled composition, ripped from my pocket and scattered all over the sidewalk. The cop, understanding, walked the remaining distance with me, asking gently for names he never got. He left me at the gate of my house and I'll never forget his words before he left . . . 'Revenge, Laddy, is sweet, but forgiveness is sweeter. The world takes care of the likes a' them.'

"And, do you know . . . it did. Calvin Ridge was shot to death a few years later by another cop during a gas station holdup; George Tucker became an alcoholic and jobless drifter who died of tuberculosis at 25; Bill Burke, who organized his own little crime syndicate, was sent up the river for twenty years and faded away; and Chester Welles was killed in a car wreck."

Goldie sighed again. "Memories of the past are painful. I think I decided my course that night: rise above those whose instinct it is to slaughter the loner, the weaker. Money, power, influence can bring it about. I shoved the crumpled pages of my composition into a bureau drawer that night. Years later, after World War II, I found it fastened in Mama's scrapbook, pages pressed out, but creases still showing. And on the last sheet . . . tear stains and a note written in her lovely hand: 'Never forget, my son, how proud you once were of your country and how proud I am of you . . . your Mama . . . ' "

The big man sniffed, stood, walked over to the bureau and pulled a book from the top drawer. Returning to the bed, he handed it to me. "Oh yes," he said, "I had a mama." It was a scrapbook, with a scruffy, tattered cover, but still revealing a little girl with faded yellow curls, sunbonnet, short dress, and a basket of daisies. Inside were an old lady's mementos. I flipped it open, found the composition and scanned the boyish scrawl made laboriously with a dip pen. Ideas plucked from a boyish mind: equal opportunity . . . two fundamental principals—respect for the individual, respect for the law . . . friendship and understanding . . . a public trust . . . a country where any people from any land are entitled to life, liberty and the pursuit of happiness. I read bits of it aloud, then gently closed the cover, glanced at Goldie who sat back on the bed, eyes closed, and turned away, my eyes misting.

Flynn's hoarse laughter broke the mood and I spun about as he now stood by the bed, chuckling and shaking his massive head. He strode over to the bureau, retrieved the two empty glasses and handed them to me.

"My God," he said, too loudly, "what driveling sentimentality. What are we, two old ladies gone senile? Go on, fix us a drink."

I stopped by the bar and ambled back to the bedroom.

"Tell me about Maria," Goldie said.

"Not much to tell. She's back in Madrid for a couple weeks."

"Made love to her yet?" Goldie leered.

"Ah . . . no . . . just good friends . . . "

"Just good friends, eh?" He fluffed through several ties. "Which one goes with the suit?"

"The blue with the white stripe. You need a woman to dress you properly."

"I've got all the woman I need." He stood before the mirror, moving his craggy head about, adjusting the tie. Then, he peeled the coat from the hanger and stalked out to the living room. I followed.

"You and Billie?" I asked.

"Let me tell you about me and Billie, Donn." He sighed and I braced myself. Was Goldie about to let down his guard and again reveal his human emotions?

"Billie and I have an arrangement. It's convenient for both of us. I met her ten, twelve years ago in New York; saved her from a rough situation. Billie's rich now in her own right. She loves the performing arts, loves to have me invest her money. I've taught her a few tricks about money, and she's taught me a few tricks."

"What's the future hold for your 'arrangement'?" I asked.

"Haaa," Flynn gurgled, fanning his mustache with a thumb. "You mean, what are my intentions? You're asking like her father, maybe?"

"No, that was phrased badly. I think a gal with all she's got would be looking for something more tangible than an 'arrangement'."

"Good ol' duty-honor-country," Goldie smirked. "You'd like to see all couples locked in holy matrimony, eh?"

"Aw, come off it."

"Well, what then? Are you interested in her?"

"I've got enough female problems, Goldie."

"Huh? You mean Maria? She's no problem—unless you make it a problem."

"My problem is that my happy marriage of twenty years is beginning to come unglued."

Goldie suddenly looked uncomfortable.

"There are more important things than women, Donn; more important than sex; that's the arms business. It's expanding so fast I can't keep up with it. I'm gonna move to Tel Aviv; set up headquarters there."

"What's the big fish fry in Israel?"

"I'm investing in an airplane plant for starters; they're gonna design and build their own fighter and I want in at the bottom. Once I establish a base there, I'll be able to move weapons and ammo and spares into the Africa market from Israel; stuff I can't do from the States or from here . . . Israel's in good with the Africans. It's gonna be a big market in five, six years; no congressional constraints in Israel."

"Sounds big."

He leaned forward and massaged his knees with beefy hands. "Look, Donn, after we tie up the Italian deal, get out of the government and tie in with me. It's too good to pass up. I'll start an account for you—nothing illegal, you understand; no conflict to sweat with all your guilt complexes. Just a numbered account in Zurich. Nobody'll know but you and me; nobody else cares. I'll place a hundred and fifty thousand dollars in it for you to draw on anytime you want . . . clean money, Donn. Think about it. Don't give me a yes or no or any preachments. It'll give you the courage—the financial guts— to quit sucking the sugar tit of government employment."

I shook my head, but he dismissed it with a wave of his hand. "No, no, don't unload duty-honor-country on me; you'll give me a guilt complex. It's done all the time. How do you think some of our mutual friends in Washington make it on a lousy government salary? A friend here or there . . . an account here or there . . . how do you think some of your own colleagues are makin' it so good— guys who never had a dime before they saw the light? Think what you could do with a hundred and fifty thousand to draw on." Flynn's face was flushed and he was sweating.

"Okay," I said, sensing my nerves tighten, "suppose I go along with the hundred and fifty thousand. How do I draw down on it? Purely hypothetical, you understand."

"All right, now you're talkin'! Here's the way it'll work: you want some money in the states, I have a special account you can draw on; you want some money here in Europe, Billie can help you. I'll get you a pass card and a number."

"Hey, hold it, Flynn," I said. "All I wanted was a hypothetical case."

He grinned. "That's about as hypothetical as I can get. Anyway, consider it. Gotta run now. Having dinner with an Eyetalian Count. Look, I'll be leaving Wednesday for Bonn. Billie knows where I can be reached." He held out a hand. "Relax and have a good time. Remember, all work an' no play makes a lotta jack!"

Goldie left Wednesday morning for Germany. That evening when I returned from the embassy, there were two notes in my key slot. One informed me that the concierge had a package for me, and the other, from Billie, invited me to tennis and dinner. I took the packet and the notes up to my room, called Billie, told her I'd be there in an hour, hung up and tore open the packet. In it was a small tape recorder, and a note which read, "Congratulations, Partner."

I fiddled with the dials and was rewarded by a reasonable transcription of my conversation with Goldie Flynn of two nights before. Only there were a few minor changes; certain words and phrases had been omitted; the tape had been doctored.

I froze as I listened to Flynn talk about the Israeli market in Africa; his offer to have me join up with him . . . "I'll start an account for you . . . a numbered account in Zurich . . . think what you could do with a hundred and fifty thousand to draw on . . . " And then, as I sat there, I heard myself say, "Okay, I go along with the hundred and fifty thousand. How do I draw on it?" The qualifying word "suppose" had been neatly edited out.

And then Goldie saying, "All right, now you're talkin'! Here's the way it'll work: you want some money in the states, I have a special account you can draw on; you want some money here in Europe, Billie can help you. I'll get you a pass card and a number . . . " There was a short pause, and then his voice again: "I'll be leavin' Wednesday for Bonn. Billie knows where I can be reached." Another pause. "Relax and have a good time. Remember, all work and no play makes a lotta jack!" The tape ran out and clicked off.

For the first minute or two, I sat there, numb. Then, I rewound the tape and played it again. Then, I picked up the card—"Congratulations, Partner." The numbness was replaced by a growing rage, first at Goldie that he would see the need to make such a tape to hold over me—obviously, to get me to push for his twenty million dollar sale of ammunition as a part of the program. He probably had several copies of this doctored tape.

Then, the anger and rage was toward myself for being a fool, a real Pinnochio, a woodenhead. I had allowed myself to be trapped into it. The fact was that I probably would have pushed for the ammo to offset all the goodies the Italians were to buy from us, without being in Flynn's hip pocket. Now, he had a second mortgage on me. I could no longer lead and direct in this area, I could only react to him, cater to him, and I didn't want to do that.

A few more moments of this and then I calmed down. What could I do? I could ignore it and go about my business and get even by trying to keep the ammo out of the package; or, I could play along with him. There was another course that I considered: Take the tape with me back to Washington and play it for Phil Barrett and discuss it with him; sort of a father and son chat, explaining how it had happened, how the tape didn't actually say what I had said. I played it once more and decided that neither Phil nor the Secretary nor anybody else listening to it would believe me. It was a real professional job of editing.

For now I couldn't do anything about it. I stood up and slipped the recorder into my brief case and tucked it away in the corner of a closet. I could only continue the negotiations. And right now that was the most important thing in my life. Meanwhile, I'd wait for

Flynn to make his pitch. Nothing else I could do about Goldie for the moment. Then I remembered Billie's invitation for tennis and dinner and it dawned on me that maybe there was something that I could do about it. I checked my watch, retrieved a bag with tennis clothes, shoes and balls, and a Davis racket strapped to the outside. I slipped on a sport coat, went to the lobby, asked the bell captain to get me a cab and headed for Billie's downtown penthouse. She wanted to play tennis; fine, I also wanted to play tennis.

She was waiting and met me in the foyer of her penthouse, smiling, poised, cool and beautiful in white tennis dress and frilly matching panties, an aluminum racket clutched in one hand, can of tennis balls in the other. "Anyone for tennis?" she asked.

I used Goldie's bedroom to change, then joined her in the sitting room. There were two courts behind her apartment and after a fast warmup we got serious.

I had played a lot of tennis in Arlington, but the constant travel, late hours, good food, and booze had put on extra pounds and slowed my agility. Billie was fast and agile, but her serve was weak. By the end of four games, it was tied, two each, and I was sweating and panting like a rutting bull. In contrast, Billie was cool and relaxed, her long legs giving her ample coverage of the court. Coupled with a controlled backhand, she spent little energy returning the ball.

I removed my shirt and began to apply the pressure. My serves were stronger and I won the fifth game. She sensed my determination and made me earn the next one, driving me from one side of the court to the other with well controlled shots. I let up and Billie took the next two games. We were tied again at four all. Then I got a second wind, bore down, charging the net and wielding a heavy racket. I took the set, six to four.

"How about another set?" I panted.

She shook her head, her face glistening with perspiration. "Send me to the showers, Coach."

I walked Billie back to the elevator and then to her suite.

"You don't like to lose, do you?" She said it as a matter of fact.

"Well, let's say I enjoy winning." I unlocked the door to her suite, pushed it open and followed her inside, enjoying her catlike grace.

She removed the white headband and wiped perspiration from her hairline.

She tossed her head back at me and smiled. "You'd make a good business partner for Goldie. He likes to win, too."

"He's won himself a beautiful woman."

She turned slowly and looked at me holding the towel away from her and there was a coolness in her voice as she spoke. "Only he hasn't won me. I don't consider myself the property of Goldie Flynn— or any man."

"I'm sorry Billie. I didn't mean it that way at all. So he didn't win you. You're still beautiful."

"Thanks, Donn." Her hand was pleasant on my arm. "I'm overly sensitive, but you know Goldie. He has one interest: the acquisition of wealth. I help him with that and he reciprocates." She walked to the window and was silent as she gazed out. "Goldie and I are much alike. We had nothing growing up; I knew what it was to be unwanted." She turned and walked back to me. "I grew up, and outwardly I became a woman, but inside I was a vulture. I wanted fame and I wanted money and nice clothes and a big car and a lovely apartment. And I got all of these. But, most of all, I wanted to be accepted."

"And you haven't been?"

"Not like I want. And Goldie is much the same. Our professions have kept us out of much of polite society."

"Aw, come off it, Billie."

"It's true. With enough money, Goldie thinks he can buy himself into any club in the country and along with it, gain political power. That's Goldie's ultimate goal. He's getting there, but it takes all of his time and a lot of his money. I want more of his time, more of his attention. I certainly don't want to be *owned,* but I want him to recognize me as a woman, not as a business partner!" Her face twisted and tears glistened in her eyes.

"Billie, Billie," I soothed, clutching her shoulders, "You are a woman, a hundred percent hunk of lovely femininity, and if Flynn fails to recognize that, the guy is blind."

I felt her relax and she turned and put her arms around my neck. "When Goldie's home—here—he spends most of his time with his papers and the telephone."

Any resistance I had, disappeared. I kissed her and she responded hungrily. Dinner was late that evening, and later, that weekend, I postponed going home. Instead, Billie and I headed for Civitavechia, the beach house, the sand and water—and the thirty-two-foot Chris Craft. We had the place to ourselves. I returned to Rome late Sunday night and caught a flight to Dulles International Airport the next day.

Chapter Nine

Trouble in Arlington

SOON AFTER MY RETURN home the gap between Cella and me widened further. Part of it, I know, was my unfaithfulness, part was concern over what Flynn might do with the tape, and part, the Italian deal which by now had become an obsession.

Uneasily I also began wondering if there was something wrong with Cella's health. Much of her stamina and zest was gone; the glowing complexion of which she always had been so proud was now pasty and almost sallow. I knew she had been to her doctor and I knew there was medication in the bathroom cabinet. I thought briefly of going to the doctor and talking to him but forgot about it in my absorption with work.

Cella diagnosed her lethargy as a need to get away from the routine of housework. I suggested two weeks at the beach with the younger kids who were wild about the idea. She and our neighbor, the wife of a colonel in the Air Force, joined forces and they left the next day with the younger children for a rented cabin at Bethany Beach, Delaware.

I was home with my two oldest boys: Bruce, preparing for his first year of college, and Kevin, preparing for the next day's fun and games—Bruce, the serious intellectual and Kevin, the free spirit. Bruce had a summer job as a lifeguard at a private pool; he also gave guitar lessons to a couple of neighbor kids in the evening, saving his money to defray part of his college expenses.

Even though I was now making the maximum salary of a civil servant, we were still strapped financially with the big house, six kids, Bruce's pending college expenses, the Tadpole's added expense. The money always disappeared quickly. Being physically removed from Goldie Flynn and his offer of an account to draw on, I was able to look at the offer in a somewhat different light. Pushing his tape recorded second mortgage to the back of my mind, the idea of some extra money had a lot of appeal. Coupled with that was the growing uneasiness that possibly Cella did have something seriously wrong that would entail expensive medical treatment.

Alone in the evening in the big house on Tazewell Street, I pondered these mounting problems and mentally searched for a solution. Occasionally the boys were home with me for dinner, but most of their evenings were taken up with friends.

One Friday morning Goldie called, exuberant as always. "I've got us a plane, Donn. Let's fly down to Ocean City for a weekend of fun and games." The plane Goldie had acquired was my ultimate dream, a Beech "V-Tail" Bonanza—a "Beecha Banana," I remembered wistfully—and it was painted a creamy yellow.

It was hard to stay angry with Goldie. And with both boys away with friends for the weekend, I was at loose ends. I met him at Page Airways in the National Airport complex about six that evening to find that he had one of the most striking platinum blondes I had ever seen, hanging onto his arm. Her name was Catherine Traynor and she had big, innocent eyes that crinkled when she laughed, which was often, and a lovely wide mouth full of orthodontally correct teeth. On the flight to Ocean City she bubbled, she effervesced, and she distracted, particularly as I let down for the Ocean City strip.

I wondered vaguely if Catherine was another present from Flynn. I also wondered what such a bright young thing saw in my rather fleshy friend who, despite the rocky ride, was dozing peacefully in the seat behind me. I wrestled the Bonanza to the ground, we parked and joined Baron and Isabel who had driven to the airstrip in a rental car to retrieve us and take us to a new motel called the Carousel.

It was a good weekend with sun, salt spray and swimming, dashing along the beach, chasing after Isabel and Catherine, reminiscent of the beach at Civitavechia. Catherine Traynor was inviting and enticing but I wasn't having any. Too costly, I reasoned. Suspecting that Goldie might have a reason for getting me involved with this blonde, I was friendly but distant to her and cool to Goldie.

The weekend was over and I flew Goldie and Catherine back to Washington Sunday night. A week later Cella returned from Bethany Beach with the children, all bronzed and rested. It was good to have them home again and things were fairly normal again.

The following Saturday I worked all day at the office and met the Baron for a drink afterwards. He had some friends and it was late evening before I got home.

Cella was reading when I stumbled in. Propped up in the big double bed, she lay there, auburn hair streaming down over suntanned shoulders. She didn't look up as I entered the bedroom.

"Hi, Love," I said softly, flipping a hand up quickly.

"Hi," she said, continuing to read.

"It's cool in here tonight."

"The air conditioning is on," she replied, turning a page.

"I know, but I have a hunch that it would be cool without it."

"Oh?"

I was muddle-headed as I sat on the bed and reached down to unlace my shoes. The leather belt cut sharply into my midsection.

"Aargh," I groaned, "must be putting on a little weight."

"If you put on any more, we'll have to reinforce the bed springs."

"My, we're a little testy tonight."

"Tonight?" She flipped the magazine onto the floor. "It's almost midnight, Donn Rodney. You said you'd be home for dinner."

"Well . . . I meant to be, but the meeting took longer than I expected."

"There was no meeting and you're drunk!"

"So I've had a few. What's eating you?"

There were tears in her eyes. "I had a special dinner tonight."

I unbuttoned my shirt, chagrined. "What was so special?"

"That!" she said, as she pointed to the dresser. Her voice broke and she turned on her side.

I walked over, puzzled. Then, I saw the huge card. It was done in bright colors, with a caricature of a grinning bulldog and a cute, long-eyelashed spaniel. "To the swellest Mom and Pop . . . " I opened the card " . . . in the whole DOG gonned world! Happy Anniversary from the pups!" And there they were; three bullpups and three little spaniels which looked a bit like girl dogs, but somebody had put a mustache on one of them. And beneath were the scrawled names of our children, and a series of lines joined together haphazardly which spelled TADPOLE.

I turned the card over and over, embarrassed. Walking to the bedside I placed a hand on her shoulder.

"Cella, baby, I'm sorry, I forgot . . . "

She shrugged off my hand and burrowed her head beneath the pillow.

"Come on, Honey," I soothed, seating myself beside her, "let me explain." I took her by the shoulders and attempted to turn her around, but she tensed her muscles, resisting.

"Leave me alone," she sobbed.

I sat there, listening to an occasional jerking sob from beneath the pillow. Minutes passed. It was quiet and I grew restless, then impatient.

"Okay, I'll leave you alone," I finally retorted. "I'll go sleep in the den."

"Go sleep with your blonde hussy!"

"Blonde hussy?" I could feel my heart quicken. "What do you mean?"

"So innocent, aren't you? What do you take me for, a fool?"

"Come off it," I said easily. "I don't know any blonde hussies."

"Oh, no?" she said, her voice rising. "Who is Catherine Traynor? One of the Sisters of the Sacred Heart?"

"Catherine Traynor?" I said lamely. "She's a friend of Goldie's."

"I'm sure that any friend of Goldie's is a friend of yours."

"Cella, you're nuts." I felt helpless, realizing suddenly that one of Cella's friends had seen us in Ocean City and done a little investigating. "Nothing at all happened between Catherine Traynor and me."

"Bull," she said, a note of finality in her voice. She pulled the covers over her shoulders and turned over with her back toward me.

"If you don't want to believe me, that's your problem," I said self-righteously. "Meanwhile, I'll sleep in the den."

She was silent. I turned out the light, walked out the door and unsteadily down the hall.

Cella took Annette and Colin to church the following morning. They returned to breakfast while, unknown to them, I lay on the glider on the screened porch, reading the Sunday paper.

"I thought you said Pop was home," Annette said.

"He is home."

"He's not in your bed, Mom. He's not in the rec room. Where is he?" Colin asked.

"He's sleeping in the den."

"I thought the den was for company," Annette said.

"Dad's company. We never see him anymore," Colin said.

"When we got back from the beach, Dad said he'd take us fishing on Sunday. That's today."

"Your father has to work extra hard now, with Bruce in college," she explained.

"Gee, when you get big and have kids, you have to work and work and there's no time for fun," Colin complained.

"I'm sure not gonna get married when I get big, Mom," Annette said.

"It will get rather lonesome unless you have somebody to share your life with," Cella said.

"I'll share it with you, Mom, and Tad. We can fish n' stuff, and you can keep our house clean."

"What about your father?"

"Oh, he can stop in when he's home."

"Then we'll take him fishin'," Colin said. "I'll be big enough to have a car and a boat and a motor, and I'll have so much tackle that Pop will be jealous, and he'll say, 'Take me fishin', Colin.' "

"And will you?"

"Sure! Pop's a real cool guy when he ain't yellin' at you."

"Do you agree, Annette?"

"Yeah," she said glumly. "Only he's not fun like he used to be. He doesn't sing those loud songs anymore or bang on the piano."

"Those are old love songs," Cella said softly, "and he doesn't bang; he plays quite well, really . . . or he used to."

"Mom, please go wake Pop up. Tell him to take us fishin'," Colin pleaded.

"All right," she said, lifting Tad from his chair. "Colin come with me and watch the Tadpole while he plays on the patio."

The children followed her outside. She came back through the screened porch and saw me lying on the glider. I tossed the paper onto the rug.

"I trust you slept well."

"Mmmrh," I grunted.

"I trust you remember you promised to take the kids fishing today."

I rolled over on the glider, propping myself up with an elbow. "You're full of trust today," I said casually.

"Gullible people keep trusting other people, even when other people may not be worthy of that trust."

"Are you 'gullible people' and am I 'other people'?"

"Are you?" she asked.

"Come over and sit down," I invited. "Let's not play cat and mouse."

"What's happened to you, Donn?"

"What's happened to you, Donn?" I mimicked. "You sound like one of the soap operas on TV. We should have some organ music."

"Donn," she pleaded, "can't you see that you've changed? You've put on nearly thirty pounds in the last few months; your face is all puffy, and the fun's gone out of you. You're always working—no time for me or the children. You never touch the piano anymore—no singing, no exercise. When is the last time you went for a run along the towpath?"

"Too long," I agreed. I was silent, reflecting. "I have put on some weight. I don't know, Cella; seems like things crowded in on me all of a sudden. There were so many deals to be made there was no time for anything else . . . no time." I pressed my eyes, attempting to erase the dull pain.

"Head hurt?" There was sympathy in her voice.

"A little."

"Leg troubling you?"

"A little."

"Conscience bothering you?"

"A little," I acknowledged with a grin.

"Don't grin at me, Donn Rodney. You can't melt me."

"It was supposed to be a smile," I said.

"With a smile like that, you should grow a mustache."

"What do you mean?"

"Then you'd look like a fox; a big, fat, sly fox! Right out of Pinnochio."

"Cella, you sure don't like me today, do you?"

She sat down slowly then on the edge of the sofa. "No, I don't like you today, nor for the last two days. But I love you—and have for twenty years; else I'd have gone home to Mother."

"Cella!"

"Don't choke up on me, Donn," she warned. "I'm not buying any of it. What were you doing at Ocean City with Catherine Traynor?"

"I was not with her or any other female," I said righteously. "I was with Goldie and Baron who had their dates with them. I slept alone."

"Somebody who saw you down there on the beach said you were making out like a high school kid at a drive-in."

I swung feet to floor and sat by her. "Look, Honey, I shouldn't have to explain anything." Her expression didn't change so I added, "But I will. Goldie has a thing going with this Traynor doll and he asked me to fly the two of them to Ocean City last weekend so I did. It's as simple as that."

"What about the making out bit on the beach?"

"Goldie is allergic to sun, so . . . ."

"Poof," she interjected. "His skin is three shades blacker than your heart!"

"No, he really is. He gets this rash. At any rate, the Traynor dame gets tried of sitting in the shade of the umbrella so she comes out and romps with me in the water."

"Romps? Describe romps!"

"Hell, no," I said sulkily. "I've had enough."

She broke then and cried great wracking sobs and I took her in my arms and comforted her. The black feeling lifted from my mind and my head no longer hurt and my leg no longer throbbed. I felt glad inside, and good; and I patted her gently on the back and told her I loved her.

Later, I took Colin and Annette fishing and we caught a few crappies and a couple of blue gills. Cella fried them for us that night.

We were sitting on the screened porch several evenings later and I could tell Cella had something on her mind. "I'm worried about Kevin," she said.

"Why Kevin?" I asked.

"Don't you notice?" There was a touch of irritation there. "He wasn't here for dinner again."

"Probably swimming late at Fort Myer."

"I want him here for dinner. He's away all day long as it is."

"Don't be concerned." I tried to soothe her. "Kevin's a good, solid kid; forgetful maybe, but good."

There was a slight smirk on her face as she said, "You're all good boys, Donn, but we girls like to know where you are and what you're doing." She paused and sighed. "Back to Kevin. I want you to talk to him."

"Okay. I'll talk to him."

And I did. It was after midnight. I was in bed, reading, waiting for the sound of the front door opening. It did—and slammed shut.

"Kevin!"

"Yeah?"

"Come in here."

"Where's here?"

"In the bedroom—where most people are at midnight." The bedroom for me was the study, but Kevin, and I imagine all the kids, knew it now as Papa's room.

He came in, looking sullen, hair hanging in his eyes.

"Where have you been all day, Kevin?"

"Swimmin'."

"Where?"

"In the water—Fort Myer."

"With whom?"

He shrugged. "Other kids." He brushed away a yellow forelock.

"The pool closes at nine, doesn't it?"

"Guess so."

"Look, you weren't home for dinner again. You're hardly ever here during the day."

"So?" He was insolent.

"So . . . !" I stopped, feeling the hackles and the blood pressure surge. It got to me. Here I was practically selling my soul to get the deal cooking in Italy to help pay for this boy's clothes, food and schooling, and he smarts off. I took a deep breath and let it out, slowly. "So, I want you home more, and I want you here for dinner—every night, understand?"

He nodded curtly.

"And don't leave the yard tomorrow—at all—or today. It is today, isn't it? Understand?"

"Yeah . . . ," sullenly.

"Kevin, buddy, come here a moment."

He shuffled to the side of the bed, hands in pocket. "Yeah?"

"Your eyes, Kevin, they're all glassy. Do you feel okay?"

"Yeah, Dad, I'm okay; too much chlorine in the water."

"Come here. Let me feel your forehead."

He grudgingly stooped down. "Satisfied?"

"Yeah, I guess so. There's ice cream in the freezer. Have some and go to bed."

He walked to the door and turned. "That's all?"

I looked at him, caught his gaze and held it.

"Kevin, laddy," I said, voice low, speaking slowly, under strain, "you are developing a snotty, hateful manner. It's not like you and I don't care for it. Neither does your mother. Try to get over it, huh? It might rub off on the little guys. You're their hero. Keep it that way, okay?"

"Uh . . . " Kevin grunted.

"One more thing: I'll be home early tomorrow night and I'm going for a run on the towpath. I want you to run with me. I'll be good for four miles. Think you can stay with me?"

"I'll be out ahead of you, Pop, all the way."

"That's my old Kevin talkin'! Good-night."

I was home at six-thirty the following evening. It was a perfect evening for running. Kevin, in track shorts and tennis shoes, was waiting for me. "Come on, Pop. I've been resting all day for this." He smiled, revealing deep dimples—Kevin the Charmer.

"Be right with you, Kev!" I said it with zest, catching the boy's exuberance that was submerged beneath the quagmire of the hostility and rebellion of the previous night.

We drove across Chain Bridge and parked by the canal. I tucked a towel around the neck of an ancient sweatshirt as we started off, jogging easily along the road paralleling the waterway. But Kevin

was like a colt let out to pasture and ran ahead with great leaps
and sudden spurts which said much what the boy would never say—
that it was good to be together, the old man and the boy; that there
was still a bond of camaraderie between us.

We switched to the towpath at the crossing—by our favorite picnic
area—and moved at a steady pace toward one of the locks in the
distance.

"Makes a man feel great, Kev."

"Yeah, you do okay for an old guy." He grinned at me.

"Thanks!" And I meant it; an occasional oblique comment of admiration from a teenager is something to treasure.

"Let's put on the gloves an' go a couple a' rounds when we get
home, Pop."

"Okay, but give me a chance to rest awhile."

"Sure, okay. I'm not goin' anywhere anyway."

Cella was agitated. I could see it in her face as I stepped into the
kitchen, feeling refreshed after a shower.

"Okay, let's have it. What's the matter?"

"Pull up a stool and read this." She placed a folded piece of paper
on the bar.

"Dear Kevin," I read. "You've got a great idea. Bring some of
the stuff with you when you come out. I figure it's good for twenty
bucks a gram here. These kids have M-O-N-E-Y! You remember the
cute blonde—Trill? She was usin' it at Radcliffe. Look, if you can't
get the old man to bring you out soon, stuff some 'way down in the
corner of an envelope. Mash it real good. I'll pay you when I see
you. I'll either peddle it or keep it for myself."

Sudden tension hurt my lips. My tongue struggled to form sounds.

"Pot!"

"What?"

"Pot—or hash, I don't know. I should have seen it!" I fought my
emotions as I stood up, feeling the throbbing in my head of constricted
arteries under pressure.

"Donn, what is it? Dope?" Cella's voice quavered, her hand groping
for mine, eyes searching for denial.

I wiped the perspiration from my face, pinching my lips, pressing them into my teeth. "Yes, dope, I guess. Marijuana or Turkish hashish, I don't know. But why Kevin, why Kevin?" I whispered, looking into the palms of my hands. And then I saw the answer, but not in my hands. It was in the nether regions of my mind and I read it clearly, sharply, and tried to scrub it out because I wasn't ready to admit it. I looked at my hands again and sighed. I flexed my fingers until they ached and made fists and studied their knuckles. I relaxed, dropped my arms and walked toward the door.

"Where are you going?"

"Kevin wanted to box. I'm going down to give him a workout."

"Careful, don't lose your cool."

With her warning in my ears, I went downstairs and into the game room. Kevin was working the bag in a steady rhythm, striking gloves on his hands.

"Ready, Pop?"

"I am if you are."

"Here, catch." He tossed me a pair of purple gloves, the big sixteen-ounce size called powder puffs. "I'll get Colin to lace us up."

While he was gone, I tugged on the gloves and pulled the yellow laces taut with my teeth, urging myself to keep cool. Kevin was too big to spank, too hateful of authority to accept a lecture, too immature for man-to-man reasoning. I tattooed the punching bag, taking the edge off my anger. Kevin and Colin burst into the room, the younger boy excited.

"Gee, Pop, can I take the winner?"

"Feel up to it?"

"Yeah, if you'll fight me on your knees. And no hittin' in the face!"

"How about Kev'? Suppose he whips me?"

"Same rules. He's bigger'n you—almost."

Colin laced our gloves.

"Okay, go to your corners," he commanded, "and, at the sound of the gong, come out fightin'!" He withdrew a pool cue from the rack and struck the metal light fixture. It clanged.

Kevin moved in, crouching, leading with his left, right fist cocked, up on his toes—light, graceful, as I had taught him. He flicked hair from his eyes, peering over a glove. I moved in, tagged him lightly, stepped back, Kevin pressed in; one-two, light blows to the chest. I danced to the side, watching, waiting. Kevin became cocky, moved

in fast, low, one-two-three. I fended off the first two, but the third
one hit hard, just above my belt.

"Good," I grunted, "good. Keep your guard up!" I moved in, pulling
my punches, got two to the body, danced back, taking a roundhouse
in the rib cage. *The kid can punch!* Pride assuaging anger. "All right,
come on, move in on me, press your advantage!"

"Bong!" Colin struck the fixture. "Time! Go to your corners."

We backed off, Kevin grinning. "Got you two good ones, Pop!"

"You're getting a real solid right, but follow it up. When you get
me off balance, move in . . . the ol' one-two. Don't hold back."

"We'd better put the guards on."

"No . . . no need."

"Okay, time's up. Get ready!" Colin hit the bell and this time I
moved in quickly. I worked in four good ones, putting a little weight
behind them, unmindful of Cella standing in the doorway but aware
of a smarting ear as Kevin caught me alongside the head. I danced
back, beckoning. "Come and get me, Kev!"

And Kevin did. He moved in stealthily, crouching, recognizing a
new severity in my punches. He lashed out, catching me on the forehead. Suddenly I stepped inside his guard and gave him a one-two
sequence in the face, snapping the boy's head back, bringing stinging
tears to his eyes. He back-pedaled, blinking, wiping his mouth with
the fat of a powder puff. "Luck!" he grunted, biting his lower lip,
danced away, beckoning.

"Come on, come on," I said. "Move in on me now. It hurt a little
huh? Get you mad?"

Kevin shook his head, blowing audibly through swelling lips and
tossing the long blonde locks from his eyes. "Nah!" But there was
hurt in his voice. He crouched, danced forward and lashed out, fanning
air. I closed, but the boy moved back and swung, connecting with
cheek bones that jarred me. Kevin followed it up with a left, driving
it into my nose.

"Good, Lad! Get mad but control it. Don't waste your punches!"

My face hurt but I liked his spirit. Don't break that spirit, I cautioned, but get the lesson across. I moved in again, rapidly pummel-
ing—left, right, left, right to the body—and quickly, a left and a right
to the face; pulled punches, but brutal, punishing. Kevin dropped
his arms, dazed, and leaned against the wall, eyes closed.

"Donn, you hurt him!" Cella was glaring at me.

"Easy, Cella," I warned. "Kev', you okay?"

He nodded grimly, raising his gloves, face working, biting a lip to still it.

"That clear the pot out of your head, Kev'?"

There was pain in his eyes and he brought his guard up, probing toward me, cocking his right, holding it close to his face, tears coursing down his cheeks. He rushed suddenly, swinging blindly, a windmill gone berserk. I absorbed most of the blows with my arms, but several broke through, raising welts on my bare chest. Twisting about, I forced him to a corner, lining him up with a chair. I drove a left to the boy's chin, sending him back into the seat where he collapsed, arms hanging limply. He began blubbering.

"Enough! Enough!" Cella was enraged as she stomped past me to Kevin. She knelt there, wiping his face with a cloth. She turned. "I hope you're happy!"

I held my gloves out to Colin. "No," I said, sighing, "I'm not."

"Gee, Pop," Colin's voice shook, "you clobbered him. You gonna clobber me, too?"

"No, Son, that's all for today."

"Hey, your hands are shakin', Pop. Did Kevin scare you? And . . . " eyes gone big, "he clobbered you, too. Your skin's all red! Gee, who won?"

"It was a draw, Colin. Nobody won."

Chapter Ten

Crisis in Arlington

SUMMER WAS ALMOST OVER; that fateful summer of 1967. Our entire family was about us again in the big brick house in Arlington. We were all together, yet further apart than we ever had been. Cella and I, cool and correct when the kids were about, formal and withdrawn when they were not. Kevin, too, steered clear of me. He was home more and with his mother more, seeming to help her about the house, willing to run errands for her and take the little kids for walks along the towpath or take Tad to the playground. Bruce was there but not there. He would leave in three days for college and was busy assembling his gear and his thoughts and saying good-by to high school friends.

We were all assembled around the dinner table that night except Tad who was sick in bed with a virus. We were discussing the Tadpole and the possibility of physical therapy for him. Bruce remarked that his avowed purpose was to teach Tad to talk and to play the guitar.

"That's very noble of you, Bruce," Kevin said.

"So what, wise guy," Bruce shot back. "Do you have any avowed purpose?"

"Only to stay out of trouble," Kevin replied.

"That, too, is noble," I said.

"It's a good feeling to have all of the knights of the round table about me again," Cella said.

"Not all, Mommy," Annette said. "Tad is a knight, too, but he's a sick knight, isn't he, Mom?"

"Yes, he is, Honey, but he'll be up in a few days."

"And then Pop will be gone," Colin said.

"Not for long this time, Colin. I'll be home in a few days and we'll fly your new model airplane," I said.

"That's a deal!" Colin exclaimed.

"Don't rescue any fair maidens when you're in Italy, Dad," Colin warned.

"He's been reading Don Quixote," Kevin explained. "I have to tell him what it's all about."

"Yeah, I don't get it. It's kind of a dumb story," Colin said.

"It's a good story. I think maybe I have something in common with Don Quixote," I said.

"Do you joust with windmills?" Bruce asked.

"Nearly every time I'm in Rome."

"I can see you now," Kevin crowed, "you and Uncle Goldie. He would be Sancho Panza."

"Why is Uncle Goldie always in Rome when you're there, Dad?" Bruce asked.

"Well, Son, he has parallel business interests. He represents several firms which are interested in defense and defense contracts."

"Mostly contracts, I bet."

"What do you mean? Goldie Flynn is a patriotic man," I said without conviction.

"But he ties his patriotic fervor to the making of a buck," Bruce insisted.

"That's what makes the world go. That's free enterprise, the capitalistic system, our way of life."

"It's pretty materialistic and mercenary."

"That may be, but it's still the best form of government on this earth."

Bruce warmed up to his subject. "Our world government teacher told us that our economy was out of balance, that our government, and others in the world, relied too much on wars. He called Korea and Vietnam and the Suez wars of convenience which are used to pep up a lagging economy."

"He sounds a little pink to me."

"Dad, you always hang a label on anybody who disagrees with you. He sounded like a sincere guy to me; kinda kooky lookin' but sincere. He thinks the Middle East thing is economic and that we are exerting our influence to heat it up."

"Why?"

Bruce shrugged. "I never asked him; good for our economy, I guess. Look at the unemployment figures. A war would bring increased production of planes, tanks, guns, munitions, create jobs, take lots of guys off the streets and put 'em in service."

"All right," Cella interjected, "I've heard enough political talk. Let's have some cheerful conversation."

"What are you gonna get Annette for her sixth birthday, Pop?" Bruce looked at his mother. "That's cheerful, isn't it?"

"I want a horse," Annette said, bouncing in her chair.

"I'm afraid it wouldn't be very practical here on Tazewell," I said.

"But you said that maybe we'd get a farm someday, Pops," she explained hopefully.

"Someday, Honey," I replied, remembering this had been a dream we all had. We had often discussed it as we drove through the Virginia Piedmont country.

"Shucks, Pops, I wanted my own horse."

"Would you settle for a puppy?"

"Gee, Dad, would I ever! My own puppy? Not Kevin's, or Colin's, or . . ."

"Your very own," I said. "Bruce will take you down to the pet shop and pick one out before he leaves for college."

"Okay, but she cleans up the messes," Bruce said.

"Oh, I will, I will!" Annette promised.

"What does Tad get?" Tad usually received a special present at all the children's birthday parties.

"I don't know. Give me some ideas."

"He's got a room full of toys."

"Yeah, but he can't see 'em very good, Pop. Why don't you bring him back a pair of eyes."

"Kevin, that's not very practical," Cella said.

"Why not? They're transplanting hearts and kidneys; why not eyes?"

"He'll get by with the ones he has—with your help, and Donnie's."

"How about something to make him hear better?" Annette suggested. "I call him and call him and he won't listen. I want him to hear me and run with me and see my new puppy."

"Maybe someday he will, Annette. For now, let's settle for one of those big, bucking horses mounted on springs. Bruce and Kevin can pick one up and teach him how to stay on."

"What's special for Mom?" Doneva asked.

"Mom will settle for lots of help and love from you children," she said.

Dessert was interrupted by the ringing of the telephone. Kevin answered it then summoned me. "It's Father O'Malley."

"Hi ya, Sean. I was afraid I'd miss you. I'm going back to Italy in a few days." I paused, listening. "Don't bother unpacking. Come on over. We'll be here all evening. See you then."

O'Malley arrived at nine o'clock. He chatted with Cella and the children, gave Tad his special blessing, helped put Annette to bed, settled an argument between Colin and Doneva, gave Kevin and Bruce some sage advice on dating, and then headed to the den with me to talk. As we walked down the stairs, a little voice trailed after me. "Pops, you forgot my kiss goodnight." It was Annette. "Yes, Hon," I answered, "I'll be there."

Down in the den Sean and I chatted aimlessly about politics for awhile, then about the arms business. The priest was disturbed about the huge arms sales to underdeveloped countries and said so. "If we live by the sword, we'll die by it," he concluded.

I shrugged. "I've heard all the arguments, Father, and it boils down to the fact if we don't sell or give military hardware to these guys, the Russians or Chinese will; or the French or the British or the Dutch, for that matter. My business may not be as pure as the work you do, but it's a moneymaking business and I'll be able to leave my boys a legacy."

"Better you leave them the legacy of a good soldier *and* a good Christian, Donn. Better a few memories of a dad who had time to go fishin' with them or listen to what's in their hearts and minds and souls in the evenin'."

"Beautiful words, O'Malley."

"I believe 'em, Gramps. If you'd spend more time at home, your boys wouldn't be slippin' into a bit of trouble."

"Easy, Sean. You're infringing on my personal domain."

"I am, am I? Haven't I always?" Father O'Malley fixed me with a steady gaze from steel blue eyes. "I have and I'll continue to do it."

I looked away. "What do you know about my boys?"

"I've one good quality you've failed to recognize, probably because you've seen so many of my bad ones," Father O'Malley said, smiling. "I'm a listener. When you're gone, I listen. Cella calls me—not to complain, you understand—but to talk. And Bruce calls me, and I listen. He's a bright lad, Donn, and he's lookin for the right way in a troubled world. And Kevin calls. That lad loves life and people and adventure! How like you they both are! They need an ear, Donn, a fatherly ear. You should be around more to lend 'em that ear."

"Bull. I've given my boys more than most!"

"Bull it is, Gramps, but it makes the grass grow green." He stood up, walked to the fireplace, then turned and faced me.

"You're neglectin' your family, Donn."

"Listen to me, O'Malley. I work my tail off for my family. I give them the good life: this house, two cars, the best schools."

"Now you listen to me, Donn," he said calmly. "There's something more important than all that and you are in danger of losing it. To hell with your fancy house and fine furniture and big cars; this house is only a shell. Give up runnin' all over the world pushing military sales. Stay here and help Cella raise your kids before you lose them. Make this house a home!"

"Bull!"

"Ahhh, your favorite expression when you know you're wrong. It's very appropriate at the moment, 'cause that's what the secular world is made of underneath the glitterin' crust . . . pure bull." He paused and sighed. "The family, Gramps . . . and your soul. Take care of them, nurture them. This earthly life is only an eye twinklin' and then it's gone."

Sean's words reminded me of my promise to Annette to kiss her good-night and I started to leave, but his comments irritated me and I stayed on to press my point.

"So, what do you want me to do?" I retorted. "Sit around and pray three times a day and read the Holy Book and waft a little incense to the air while my family starves?"

"No, Lad, not at all." His voice was gentle and he eased back in the chair, reached for a cigar and slowly unwrapped the cellophane. "Just ask the Lord for a little faith; give Him a little trust."

I drifted to the bar, looking for what had come to be my fortitude— a stiff drink. I reached for a bottle and flipped up a couple of clean glasses. "Guess I have slipped some over the years, Sean."

O'Malley rose from his chair and moved to the bar where he could keep eye contact with me. "We all slip, Gramps. Why don't you slip back up?"

I poured a couple fingers of Scotch in one glass. O'Malley shook his head when I started to pour him one. "I'm not sure I want to," I admitted. "The pace of this world is so frantic and there's so much I have to do." I stared at my drink morosely. "I suppose we all need to go back to those simpler days."

"You can't go back, Donn." He spoke softly and his big hand was light on my shoulder.

"No, we can't. Maybe that's what I'd really like to do; go back . . . or escape . . . "

"Escape back to your family, Donn. They need you and you need them."

"I'd like to, Father, but . . . " I stopped, then plunged ahead, "it just seems that Cella has lost interest in me as a husband; she loves her own life better—the kids and all—and her tennis friends and her do-gooder projects. There's no time for me. In Rome there is a lot of temptation . . . "

O'Malley's eyes were gentle yet unwavering. "Temptation . . . a part of life . . . always that way, Gramps. The snake tempted Eve. Lucifer tempted Christ in the wilderness. All through the ages we've had the temptress. It's part of God's plan, nonetheless . . . no man is immune—including a priest—we just pray harder." He chuckled.

"Sean, I don't pray at all." I found myself confessing. "I work on my negotiations and when I have a free moment, I look about for some diversion . . . someone soft, warm, compassionate. Can I stop? Do I want to?" I shook my head. "O'Malley, maybe you should give me a little of your fortitude."

"Donn, friend, I scarce have enough for myself. I've slipped too, in my day. Each day I ask God to give me the grace, the forbearance not to fall again. Do you think I don't know temptation! Once, I was set to leave the church, Gramps, to chuck the role of cleric; my life for thirty years . . . for what?"

"O'Malley," I said, now thick-tongued, "say no more. You tripped, but you're on your feet. You're walkin' tall. Pull me up, pull me up, and we'll walk together."

"Sure I will, Gramps. We're a couple of sinners, but never forget, Christ loves the sinner as well as the saint." The big priest put his arm around my shoulders.

And then we both heard the clump . . . clump . . . clump . . . thud!

We looked at each other, shocked. The frightened cry of a child catapulted us forward.

O'Malley shoved me through the door to the recreation room, where we saw the child at the bottom of the stairwell, a small crumpled heap in a blue nightdress.

"Tad!"

But it wasn't Tad. The hair was blonde and curly. It was Annette and her head was twisted at an angle. I seemed to float the ten feet to her, knelt to scoop her up when I felt the strong pressure on my shoulder.

"Easy, Gramps. Don't lift her!" The voice conveyed an awful urgency. I nodded dumbly as Annette's eyes fluttered open. Relief surged through me.

"She's okay, Father!"

"Don't pick her up!" The priest reached for a phone as Cella flashed down the stairs, a low moan escaping from her. She knelt by the six-year-old and I held a restraining hand to her arm.

"Hello, operator: an emergency. Get me the Arlington Rescue Squad." His voice was low, authoritative.

Then Annette raised a tiny hand. "Pops . . . you forgot . . . kiss good-night . . ."

"Annette, I was comin' up . . ." My voice broke. I held the little hand in one of mine and my wife's in the other and we looked at each other and I saw the fear in her eyes. From a great distance, I heard the voice of the priest, calm, assured, giving directions to the rescue squad . . . "child fell down stairs . . . possibly a broken neck . . ."

"Pops . . . can I . . . my very own puppy . . ."

Chapter Eleven

Return to Rome

As FATHER O'MALLEY, Cella and I hunched tensely in the speeding ambulance, I stared numbly at my daughter's pathetic little figure on the stretcher. While O'Malley and Cella prayed, memories raced through my mind: of a laughing little bundle of energy whom we named Annette Reneé because we wanted a cuddly French doll. Instead, for six years, she had been a Norwegian tomboy who had learned to catapult herself into the middle of family scenes to get attention. Her ruddy freckled face was now pale, her bright blue eyes cloudy with fear and pain, her curly blond hair limp on the pillow.

She was wheeled into Arlington Hospital and examined while the three of us waited uncertainly. A young doctor gave us the news gently. Annette had a broken neck. Cella sobbed and clung to Father O'Malley. I cursed the fate that would allow this to happen to my child. An hour later a nurse let us tiptoe into her room. Annette was asleep, breathing quietly—a tiny figure in a cold, white, sterile bed. We kissed her good-night and went home to wonder: Would she ever regain the use of her limbs, not just to run and play but to brush her teeth and feed herself?

Barrett agreed to postpone the Italian negotiations another week while Cella and I stationed ourselves in the hospital. X-rays had revealed the fracture; there was paralysis and possibly severe damage to the spinal cord. Her neck and upper body were placed in a plaster cast while the doctors refused to give us any prognosis for the future. They did prepare us for a long hospitalization, however.

I still didn't want to go back to Rome, but there was nothing I could do for my daughter except sit beside her hospital bed. A week passed. Annette showed faint movements in her toes and the doctors were more hopeful. I cabled Barrett, who was already in Italy, that I was on my way.

During the flight from Dulles to Rome I couldn't sleep, so I drank. It was eight hours of introspection, asking myself a multitude of unanswerable questions, digging up old memories of happier times with my wife and children.

A lovely and efficient stewardess with a head of platinum hair was serving us dinner. I caught her looking at me with a troubled expression. After the rush of serving and when the other passengers had settled down to read or sleep, she brought me a pillow and slipped it behind my head. Then she sat beside me. Incredibly, her name was Annette, and I told her about my Annette. She was a marvelous listener. But she was more than that. She was filled with the love of living and the love of people. Words and ideas flowed from her in an air of goodness and wholesomeness. As the Boeing 707 droned over the Atlantic, we sat in virtual isolation in the rearmost seats by the galley, talking of many things far into the night and later— after midnight—she taught me the twenty-third Psalm. *The Lord is my shepherd, I shall not want. He maketh me to lie down in green pastures . . .*

I must have dozed, but I remember her kiss, gentle as a rose petal on my cheek as she left. And much later, for we were over Portugal and I caught the dawn's rosy hue etched across the stratus, she was back with a breakfast tray and a warm smile. There was a folded piece of paper on the tray which I read and placed in my billfold— the twenty-third Psalm in her handwriting. Later, after breakfast, I pressed my face against the rounded glass of the window and gazed at the brightening sky above and the rolling cumulus below and I tried to pray but couldn't find the words. Am I trying to make a deal with God to restore my Annette? Am I trying an arms peddler's technique with God? *You scratch my back, Lord, and I'll scratch yours?* I extracted the folded paper and reread the Psalm, but now it brought no comfort.

From the Rome airport I took a cab to the Terrista Hotel off the Via Venetto. Flynn and Billie Mason and General Saragati owned the place, I had discovered recently, and now I always got a suite for the price of a single. It was so convenient . . . and wrong? What's wrong with taking advantage of a good deal? I was back in another world: the secular world where right always gave way to convenience, where loyalty always reigned over honesty, where pragmatism was king.

And Phil Barrett was there; the super salesman himself—all smiles and so solicitous about my daughter. The negotiations had come to life again, and that first day he deferred to me and treated me warmly, which was quite something for Phil Barrett, since I was neither God, the President, nor the secretary of defense.

But I was grateful, nonetheless, and also grateful to have somebody as artful as Barrett to smooth talk General Saragati who was personally handling the tank deal for the Italian minister of defense. Things seemed to be coming to a head in this on-again, off-again program and now I finally sensed victory.

So did our colleagues, the cat and the fox—or as Barrett called them, "the Gold-Dust Twins," Baron and Flynn. They were jovial that night at a party given by the ambassador. Why not? The Italian deal was about to be consummated and they would each make a great deal of money.

But Phil Barrett cautioned us not to become overly optimistic; there was still the German problem. An Italian faction, powerful army generals, wanted the German Leopard tank and were pushing for it. However, it seemed almost certain that we would still get the deal, only it would cost a bundle and would take the combined resources of state, CIA, and defense to bring it off. I was ready to do anything to make it happen. We did have an ace in the hole: the shah of Iran wanted four hundred M-47 tanks rebuilt. We could direct that business to the Italians. Instant profit! The Italians understood instant profit. My pulse rose each time I thought of the stakes ahead.

But I was still cool and formal toward Goldie when we met again in Rome. The threat of the second mortgage he held over me was bitter in my mouth, and I think he sensed it. The weekend at Ocean City hadn't restored the old relationship; if anything it had made me more wary of him than ever before. He had heard of Annette's fall and when he grasped my hand in both of his, there were tears in his eyes and his lip trembled.

"Donn," he said. "I talked with Cella this afternoon and she'll be calling back at ten. Be in your room at ten each night while you're here and she'll give you a report. Talk as long as you like; it's part of the room service."

I shook my head, unable to speak. I wanted nothing from this guy who would sell out his own mother. "Lemme handle my own calls," I said.

"Come on, old friend," he insisted. "Don't hold that tape recorder against me. I'd never do anything to hurt you."

A vision of his colleague stepping out of a fifth floor hotel window flashed through my mind and I remembered the phrase, "It only hurts for a little while."

The following night, I reached Doneva at home in Arlington and she was exuberant. Annette had awakened that day and wanted ice cream! "She's gonna be okay, Pop; it's because we've been praying for her. Are you praying for her, Pop?"

"Yes, Donnie," I lied. "I am praying for her." And I hung up and broke down. I sat on the bed, head bowed, but no words came, so I turned to my twenty-third Psalm and read it twice.

Later that night, we gathered in Phil Barrett's suite at the Cavalerri Hilton to go over last minute plans on the Italian package which now contained a provision to buy ten million dollars in ammunition from the Italians as a concession for all the weapons they were to purchase from us. I began to breathe a little easier. This should certainly sweeten the deal. The ammo was to be used for what we called "off-shore procurement." We would buy it from the Italian munitions maker and ship it to some of our grant-in-aid countries who were still on the dole receiving outmoded weapon systems, as well as spare parts and ammunition from us.

I could sense that Goldie Flynn was pleased over the provision, but there was something else about Flynn. There had been times in recent days when I had wanted to punch him out for the tape deal. But I recalled his vivid accounts of growing up poor in the Kansas City junk yard; his attachment to a loving mother; his grade school composition and what he called "the second crowning." I found myself sympathizing with him more than hating him. And yet, there was a curious foreboding about it, as if there was some terrible conflict going on inside him.

I noticed it that night in Phil Barrett's suite as we discussed strategy. Goldie was introspective, almost melancholy, and was drinking Coca Cola; I couldn't remember the guy without a scotch in his hand. I knew he loved my daughter, Annette, and wondered if he, as well as I, was suffering with her.

As a diversion from the constant talk of negotiations, we switched to the ongoing war in Vietnam. During the summer, Barrett had been to Vietnam and now, as he sat back in the lounge chair, he gave us a rundown. There had been a stir in the United States about a group of U.S. soldiers moving into a village and shooting a group of unarmed civilians. Barrett shrugged as he mentioned it, stating that these kinds of things were bound to happen where a shooting war is going on.

"Yeah," Goldie said, "I know from experience during the Big War. People get killed in a war: women, some old and ugly, some in the flower of youth; babies, some nursing at the mother's breast; toddlers, two and three-year-olds; little boy babies, little girl babies . . . cuddly, smiling, laughing, gurgling bits of warm, pulsating flesh and blood . . ."

"All right, Flynn," the Baron said, irritated. "Most of us know what a baby is."

"Ah, but you've never had one . . . I've never had one." He grinned at me. "Donn's had enough for all of us. I've never had a boy come running to me, arms outstretched, calling, 'Daddy, Daddy . . . ' "

"Make your point." There was a gruffness about the Baron.

"No point." Goldie shrugged. "I was just thinking what a stink we make about a soldier shooting a civilian. Well, lemme give you a statistic; we've killed over two hundred thousand civilians in the Vietnamese thing so far, mostly with bombs—five hundred pounders, seven hundred fifty pounders; I've sold a passel of 'em; and fighter aircraft strafing twenty and forty millimeter rounds. Good profit there if you sell 'em in quantity."

"You're drifting a bit, Goldie," Phil Barrett said. "We were talking about an isolated incident in Vietnam where armed soldiers shot unarmed civilians."

"Ah, but what am I talking about?" There was a sort of Satanic glee about Flynn. "Of course, I'm talking about death by remote control. We bomb cities and villages and strafe huts and set them afire, but—and here is the saving grace," he waved a pudgy forefinger slowly.

"The distinction! We were on a mission; bombing from twenty thousand feet, strafing from a thousand or even five hundred; too far away to recognize whether we were getting a twenty-year-old female or an eighteen-year-old gook with a burp gun, or an almond-eyed girl of six. But, what the hell's the difference . . . they're all the enemy."

"Aw, come off it, Goldie; for God's sake, whatsa matter with you tonight? Have a drink!" Baron slapped a fat hand against the top of the cocktail table.

Goldie was wide-eyed, all innocence. "Nothing's the matter. I'm just talking about the end product of our business—our chosen field. Weapons are for war . . . war is for killing. You should know, Baron; you had two years in the armored corps, didn't you?"

"That was the war that saved democracy," Baron said. "I was proud to be in that war."

"You mean you wouldn't be proud to serve in Vietnam?"

"Hell, I'd serve, but it's the wrong war at the wrong time."

"Hey, where's your national spirit? We're in there fighting for God and country, defense of democracy, freedom for mankind, to prevent the insidious spread of communism . . . "

"Gott mit us." Phil Barrett said it and laughed quietly.

"Of course," Goldie said. "The emblem on the German storm trooper's belt buckle as he marched in defense uff der Vaterland."

"Well, we ain't exactly defending our vaterland over there in gookland," Baron said.

"Well, what are we doing? We're killing the enemy . . . three thousand in one week, five thousand in another. That is, if we can believe the body counts. And we lose a few of our own; thirty one week, fifty another; our boys killed. God, what a loss! Prime of manhood, all those fine young American boys. But, we are making the world free for democracy!" And here Goldie paused and looked about. "And a few of us, including every man here in this room, are making more money than we ever thought possible. Stop the war? Hell, no. Kill the golden egg-laying goose? Never! Every bomb dropped is a thousand dollars worth of business, every one-o-five round fired, ninety-five dollars. Hell, even an M-16 round is worth thirteen cents. We lose a plane: two million bucks for a replacement, a million for a helicopter. Dear Lord, what a gold mine!"

"You've drifted from your point," Phil Barrett said dryly.

"No, I'm leading up to it. The guys who shot the unarmed civilians; they weren't twenty thousand feet up. They were twenty feet away, and they strafed—not with twenty and forty millimeter rounds, but just little dinky, souped-up twenty-twos with bullets costing thirteen cents apiece. They killed two, three civilians and, my God, how our lawmakers pontificated: horrible, abhorrent, sickening; and the press picked it up and blew it up. How could brave, American fighting men do such inhuman, animalistic acts as to kill noncombatants, old men, young women, mothers, babies, children . . . dear Jesus, how could this be?"

"Dear Jesus could tell 'em we've been doing this since time began," Baron said.

"Yes, He could. But, now, we're civilized, we do it now within established parameters, within the 'Rules of Warfare.' 'Men, you may kill as many women and children as you like, as long as you cannot see them physically, as long as you cannot see their pleading eyes or upheld arms or hear their begging cries. Kill them and count them— at least give us an estimate for higher headquarters. For this is war and they are the enemy. And for a reward, we will decorate you and place you on a pinnacle and your name shall be revered forever. But,' " and here Goldie' s voice rose to a crescendo, and he was sweating, " 'kill one of the same in the open and you will be vilified by all humanity!' "

At this point, Barrett became agitated. He stood up and paced about. "But, Goldie, you fail to make a distinction. It is abhorrent to me . . . to any thinking man . . . to shoot a defenseless woman or child deliberately."

"But, why this distinction?" Goldie asked, speaking calmly, a slight smile on his face. "A child is dead as quick from a piece of metal from a thousand pound bomb dropped from twenty thousand feet as he is from a twenty-two slug fired from twenty feet. Why should there be a distinction?"

Now Phil Barrett retrieved the élan and polish of the Eastern Establishment intellectual and brought forth a bit of logic, perhaps from one of his early Harvard law courses. "It is the nature of man to make a distinction," he said, "and it is this very distinction that advances civilization. The public reacts with apathy to a remote war in a remote place; there are protests, yes, but with limited effect. But a story with pictures and eye-witness accounts of a brutal murder of an unarmed civilian by a soldier? This becomes personal. You and I can identify. The public is no different today than it was at the time of Christ when Seneca said . . . how did it go . . . 'We are mad, not only individually but nationally. We check manslaughter and isolated murders. But what of war and the much vaunted crime of slaughtering whole peoples?' It's human nature to object to a killing, just as it is human nature to tolerate a war."

"Gott mit us," concluded Goldie, downing his Coke.

The session broke up shortly after that. Just before stepping out the door, Goldie stopped and turned to me. "Say Donn," he said, "did you know about Maria?"

"No. What happened?"

"She's getting married; just heard it yesterday. To some fellow in Madrid."

I stared at him. He looked just as puzzled as I felt, then turned and left.

I headed back to my hotel and to bed, my mind whirling. Maria? What *had* happened? And then I told myself it was really none of my business. She was a free person, able to do as she pleased, and I was a married man with six kids.

Annette. My mind was at rest about her now; she was getting the best of care from competent doctors, a solicitous mother and the attentive Father O'Malley. Sean O'Malley; I wished my big Irish friend was with me at the moment so we could talk.

What was it he said about marriage; it takes three? Wasn't two enough? I had certainly loved Cella. Now something was wrong. But I refused to believe the problem lay solely with me.

Someone laughed heavily in the hotel corridor as they passed my room and I thought of Goldie Flynn. He hadn't been laughing tonight; his somberness was unreal and his almost peacenik blatherings were so out of character. What had happened to him? Was he heading for a breakdown of some sort? Then I laughed at the irony of it; with Goldie holding a second mortgage over me, I should want to kill him. Yet here I was feeling sorry for him.

I couldn't sleep. I got up from the bed and walked to the window and looked out at the night. Annette faded in, and then her mother— my wife—standing by her . . . the two of them there, an almost overpowering feeling. I shook my head clear and stumbled back to the bed.

And then, a strange thing: something I hadn't done since a child in the attic of the old Dakota farmhouse. I knelt by the bed and bowed my head upon the bed. "Lord," I said, "bless and protect Annette and Ursella; give them strength and vigor and health. Restore them, make them whole . . ."

I crawled under the sheet and drifted off to sleep.

Chapter Twelve

Return to Civitavechia

FRIDAY CAME AND WE were making further progress with the Italians. Phil Barrett and I were elated as we broke up the meeting at the ministry of defense and headed back to our hotel. "Let's enjoy the weekend," he said, "take off, get away. I'm going to Milan. We'll get together Monday morning at the embassy."

I went to my room and placed a call for my home in Arlington to check on Annette's condition. While I waited for it to go through, I debated whether to go out for dinner or have one sent up. The telephone rang. It was the Baron; he wanted me to join him for a weekend on the beach at Civitavechia. Goldie and Billie were in Bonn and he and Isabel wanted company. "Come on," he urged, "you need to get away. I just signed a contract with Agusta Helicopter. I wanna celebrate; we'll lie in the sun and fish from the boat."

Civitavechia. It stirred up memories of Maria. And later Billie.

"Okay, Baron. I'd like to go; when are you leaving?"

"About an hour from now."

"An hour's okay; my call home should come through before then."

"No fancy clothes—beach wear, maybe a sport coat in case we wanna eat out."

The phone rang again as I was dressing. It was morning in Arlington and Doneva was on the line. She was home from school with a cold; Cella and Father O'Malley were at the hospital with Annette who was better, eating solid food, moving her legs. If she continued to improve, she would be released in a couple weeks. How is everybody

133

else? I asked, and Donnie said fine, everybody's fine. "How are you, Pop?" And I said, fine, and she said, "I'll tell Mom you called."

A few moments later, the phone buzzed again. It was the Baron. "We're down in the lobby, Donn. Let's roll; we'll get in a swim before dark."

I grabbed a bag and hurried to the elevator. As the door slid back on the main floor and I walked out, I saw her standing by the reception desk, the long black hair cascading about trim shoulders. She was dressed in a white two-piece suit with a bright green scarf around her throat. It was Maria.

She smiled at me, white teeth flashing. "Are you surprised?"

"Yes," I said, "surprised and glad." I was also shocked at her appearance: a haunting beauty about her, but one of fragility heightened by the pronounced cheekbones and sunken cheeks.

The Baron stood nearby, a wide grin across his face. "Didn't know you two knew each other," he said.

"Pooh," Isabel said. "Hello, Donn. We know each other." She kissed me and it was pleasant, but I was dazed by this other woman who I thought had faded from my life.

We piled into the Mercedes, the Baron and Isabel in front and Maria and I isolated in the rear, separated from the front by a pair of folding jump seats.

"Maria," I said, "what about . . ." But she touched my lips with cool fingertips. "Don't, Donn," she said. "Later, the questions . . . maybe some answers . . ."

The Baron was efficient. He had called ahead and Juanita had a lavish meal ready for us. It was too late to go for a swim, so we ate and then Baron and Isabel went down to the dock for a moonlit boat ride. Maria and I went into the little used sitting room where she glided to a stereo and found a tape of Guy Lombardo which set the mood. She perched primly on the edge of a French love seat and I sat on the carpet nearby.

"There have been questions in your eyes all evening, Donn," she said.

"You said there would be answers. What comes first?"

"Well," she laughed, "it is usual to ask first the question, but I think I know your questions."

"You're ahead of me then. I'm not sure I know them. To me you have always been the question."

"I don't know if I like that." She frowned and then washed it away with a smile, leaning toward me and taking my hand in both of hers. "You think I am an enigma?"

"Yes, as long as I've known you."

"That's maybe the trouble," she said, twisting on the sofa to face me, still clutching my hand. "I didn't want to know you too well."

"Why not?"

"Afraid I might like you too much."

"That's a straightforward statement."

"Oh, I can be, sometimes, Donn. You are always open. Not like Goldie or the Baron. They are closed and secretive; you can never read them, but I am like them. It is good for defense. You can't get hurt."

"Remember when we first met?"

She nodded slowly, green eyes holding mine. She drew one leg beneath her, glancing down briefly to smooth the white nylon skirt.

"Maria," I said, leaning away from her against the arm of the sofa, "why were you at the party in London that night?"

Her eyes clouded and she withdrew her leg from beneath her and fiddled with the strap of a gold sandal. "I was invited."

"By whom?"

She looked at me. "Does it matter?"

"To me, it does."

"Where were you on the night of May the sixteenth?" She mimicked the rough tone of my voice and we both laughed.

"Did Goldie Flynn invite you to the party?" I asked.

She nodded, then reached down to loosen the offending sandal and kick it away.

"Why?" I tried to keep my voice gentle.

"To meet you," she said.

"Was it sort of a business arrangement, Maria?"

She looked at me and there was hurt in her eyes and she reached down to unfasten the other sandal. She retrieved both and placed them on the cocktail table.

"Too many questions?" I asked. "So far not too many answers."

"I didn't expect that kind of question." Her voice was constricted.

"What kind did you read in my eyes?"

"Something like 'why are you here, Maria?' or 'why are you not home and married in Madrid?' "

"Okay, why aren't you home and married in Madrid?"

"There were too many shadows in the way," she said, shrugging gently.

"Shadows?"

"Yes . . . and impediments." She pressed fingers to her eyes and then looked at me. "You were one of the shadows."

"Shadows?" I was puzzled. "Is that good or bad?"

"Many times, I asked myself that same question. Good for your ego, maybe, to think I would remember you when you were gone. You were always a shadow on my mind." She shrugged and arched her eyebrows. "Did you ever think of me when we were not together?"

"Yes," I said.

"Even when you were home with your wife?"

"Yes."

"You never told me you were married."

"You never asked."

"And that you have many children."

I shrugged. "Marriage equals children . . . good marriage equals many children."

"And your marriage . . . it is good?"

"It was once . . . now, no."

"With so many children you must be Catholic, eh? You have six, no?"

I nodded. "With so many children I must be Catholic or careless. I was a Catholic. I was also a Lutheran. Now . . . well, I am not much of anything. I think sometimes I would like to be a Christian, but my flesh is too weak. I like too much of the material things of the world."

"Ahhh," she said, arching her eyebrows. "To be a Christian you must be pure and good? Then there are no Christians in this world."

"Maybe not," I said, suddenly uncomfortable. "But here I am answering your questions. You were going to provide me with answers."

She laughed and stood up. "Come, fix yourself a drink and let's go out on the patio."

"No thanks, Maria. With you, I don't need a drink."

"Is that good or bad?"

"Depends," I said, laughing. "Good for your ego, maybe."

"*Touché,*" she said, sliding back the door to the patio. We stepped outside and the cool, night air enveloped us. Our eyes became accustomed to the darkness and we found a glider and sat down and soon the stars came into view.

"A good night for memories," I said.

"Yes," she said, "I remember that night on the boat here at Civitavechia."

"I remember especially that night," I said. "The stars were much like tonight."

"And later, we walked back here to the cottage. You left me in the hall. After I was in my bed, I wondered if you would come to my room."

"I thought about it."

"And yet, you didn't."

"No."

"I don't understand."

"Nor I. Tell me, did you want me to come to your room that night?"

She looked at me and I could see the reflection of stars in her eyes. "No, I really did not want you to. But I thought you would."

We were silent for a while. "There is another memory," I said. "The day we went on the picnic: a beautiful day."

"Yes, a special time . . . a special place . . ."

Her fingertips gently touched my cheek. "I'm glad it was the way it was."

"Was Goldie glad?" I regretted that I said it, but it was too late.

She stiffened and drew away. "Why . . . what do you mean . . . Goldie?"

"Did Goldie give you a small tape-recording cassette?"

She was silent and I could see her sitting upright—a silhouette on the edge of the glider. I reached for her hand, but it was lifeless and slowly she withdrew it.

"I'm sorry, Maria. Perhaps I was too blunt." I pulled back to the opposite end of the glider.

"Ah, but that is you too, Donn. Maybe blunt, but maybe honest too, eh?" She sighed and I could see the shadow of her hand push a strand of hair. "Yes. It had been on my conscience for so long a time. Yes, I was to make a recording for Señor Flynn."

"Why?"

"Because he wanted it. Because it was Goldie Flynn who kept my father in funds in Rome. Goldie took care of my father—my drunken father who was cut off from the Valdez fortune. Goldie supplied him with a livelihood in turn for favors, not the least, the favors of his daughter."

I sighed audibly and stretched out my legs.

"So, now you know," she said. "Not so pretty picture, no? And what do you think of me . . . now?"

"I think you are a warm, wonderful woman . . . and I . . . I like you . . . very much." I had trouble getting it out and my voice cracked; and I could make out her silhoutte, leaning forward, face in her hands. Then I heard the stifled sobs and I moved closer and laid my hand on her back, at the nape of her neck, under the wealth of hair, and I could feel her shoulders shaking. She leaned toward me, her head feeling for my shoulder and she lay against it, sobbing quietly and I patted her back as I would a small child's.

We heard the Baron's booming voice then, and Isabel's laugh, as they returned to the cottage. Maria stood up suddenly. "Oh, I don't want to see them," she whispered. "I'll see you in the morning . . . for breakfast. Don't think so bad of me!" She fled into the house.

Since I had no desire right then to talk to either the Baron or Isabel, I followed. I heard Maria's footsteps moving up the stairs and I followed discreetly, locating the room Isabel had assigned to me. I softly shut the door, undressed and crawled into bed. Sleep came slowly. It was a night of soft shadows, memories and unanswered questions. Maria was different; she was lovely; she was an enigma. She was here and so was I, and home was four thousand miles away. I dozed.

Something awakened me. I heard muffled noises from Maria's room. I threw back the sheet, slipped on a bathrobe I found in the closet and soft-footed across the rug to my door and out to the hall. Her door was ajar and now screams struck me full force. Quickly, I strode into her room. Maria was hysterical. She sat on the edge of her bed, clad in a light blue negligee. Doña Isabela was trying to console her.

Maria was screaming and ranting. Striding over, I jerked her upright and slapped first with the palm, then the back, the palm and the back . . . slap, slap, . . . sharply but not too hard. Her face jerked one way, then the other, and after a few gasps she was quiet.

"Please, Donn," Isabel pleaded, holding my arm back, "that's enough!"

I was conscious of Maria's look of horror, her eyes big, blood oozing from a nostril and her upper lip puffing out. I sat down beside her and she leaned against me, resting her head on my shoulder.

"I'll be in my room." Isabel moved regally across the rug and out of the door, closing it softly behind her.

Every light was on in the bedroom. I moved over to a chair alongside the television. "Go to bed, Maria. I'll stay here until you fall asleep."

She sat on the bed, pulling one leg beneath her, looking at me, a silken strand of hair falling over one eye. She brushed it aside. "I don't know what happened . . . I sort of know, but I don't know why." She buried her face in her hands.

Knowing that I was near an explanation, I bore in. "You're full of hate inside: for me, your father, any man; and you mask it, and very well, too, with your Spanish beauty and your Spanish charm, and your Spanish temper. You're a Spanish queen, all right . . . you're also a Spanish bitch!"

"No, no, no," she shook her head violently, speaking painfully through tumescent lips. "Don't, Donn, don't . . ."

"What's wrong with you, Maria? You've got so much that's good and beautiful . . ."

"I'm not good and I'm not beautiful. I am a bitch. I don't hate you, Donn. I—I hate myself."

"Bull."

"It's true," she moaned quietly. "It's honest-to-God true." She looked at me, shaking her head slowly.

She came over and stood next to me, one hand on her mouth. "You beat me up," she said, surprised. "You really did! My nostrils are caked with blood . . . and a fat lip. See, bruised inside. You are a bully!"

"I'm sorry, Maria. I didn't mean to slap so hard. You were hysterical . . ."

"I know, I know, I had it coming." She laid a cool hand on my forearm. "You should have punched me right in the nose, Donn." She grabbed my hand and shaped it into a fist and pressed it against her nose: "Like that! Pow!" She laughed, but it was cut off by a choke, and tears rolled down her cheeks.

She strode over to the bed, standing there with her back to me. "Donn, no more games. I'm tired . . . tired of running away . . . running away from myself."

"Why do you run, Maria?"

"Because I'm a leper . . . inside. I feel dirty. I have always felt dirty. I think maybe it is my soul that is dirty, so I pray . . . maybe too much, and I seem to be better. But then, when I get into a predicament . . . with you . . . with the man I almost married, something happens. I want so badly to give myself; I tried so hard at the picnic, but something comes over me, a terrible guilt. Then I go away and pray. Maybe, instead of asking for God's forgiveness, I should ask yours."

"Not mine, Maria," I said, moving to her side. "Maybe we both should pray." And then I halted, standing there, suddenly seeing my image in the mirror, and I laughed, eyeing the character who laughed back; a figure in a too small bathrobe that hardly reached to my knees.

She came over and sat at my feet. "What is so funny?"

I let out a long sigh. "Nothing . . . everything . . . after all these months I see you and then beat you up."

"Nooooo," she moaned, holding her face in her hands. "No, you only beat some sense into my head."

"All right," I shrugged. "Beat some sense into you . . . and now, about to pray with you. Pray! My God, what hypocrisy!"

She sat there with her arms about my legs, chin resting on my knee, looking up at me, suddenly gentle, little girl-like. "All right, let's pray."

I was silent and shook my head.

"Donn," she said, voice low, insistent, "you have faith, I can tell." As I shook my head, she continued, "But you're human too, and I'm human! There must be some good in our meeting and knowing each other. Everything doesn't have to be all bad and wrong, does it? Surely, if there is a God, He must understand!" She was pleading now and I felt totally inadequate.

"Look, Maria, I'm Donn the arms peddler, not John the Baptist. I don't know anything about prayers. I wish I did. If I'd paid more mind to my own religion, if I'd inherited a bit more of my father's faith . . . Look Maria, it's nearly two o'clock; another place, another time for prayers."

"All right. Turn off the lamp, but leave a light in the bathroom. I don't like the dark. And stay just a few minutes more."

I clicked off the light, pulled the chair close to her bed and groped for her hand.

"Why?" I asked.

"Why, what?"

"Why are you afraid of the dark?"

She was quiet for a time. Then setting her mind to it, she recited in a low monotone: "When I was sixteen, I was living in Spain with my aunt and uncle. Doña Carlotta, my aunt, died. Don Carlos took it so very hard and drank too much. Then, one night—it was quite late—came a knock on my door. It was my uncle, drunk. He came in and said he wanted to kiss me good-night; he bent down and he . . ." She stiffened and rolled away from me. "He—he slobbered all over me and called me Carla . . ." She choked up. I clutched her hand in both of mine and squeezed it.

"Then what, Maria?"

She swallowed several times, moving her head from side to side on the pillow. "He fumbled around for me under the covers, then took off his pants and crawled under. My God." She tore her hand from mine and sat up quickly, swinging her feet to the rug and clutching her stomach.

"Sick?"

"No, I'll be all right."

"I'm sorry I made you remember."

"I never forgot! I—I wanted to tell somebody for so long. It was like a dream. I knew I'd awaken, but it was real. I could feel him and smell him, and I wanted to scream, but nothing came out . . ." She shuddered and tugged at her hair.

"No more, Maria!"

"Yes, I'll tell it all! I must, I must!" She twisted loose and stood up, pacing on the rug, her voice a fierce whisper. As she talked, great tides of pity and guilt washed over me.

"He bored into me, like . . . like shoving a stick into a sack of flour, and he worked at it, frothing and groaning. I wanted to die. I couldn't get away . . . I hurt. God, how I hurt . . . and I passed out, and when I came to, he was gone. I knew I must be dreaming, but I wasn't. I wanted lights . . . lights!" She choked again and whimpered like a child.

"Maria . . . easy . . . easy . . ."

"I could hardly walk to the light switch. I couldn't find it! I groped and tried to scream and . . . absolutely nothing. I was petrified. I finally found it and the light was there and I was there, and I could tell he had been there . . ."

I stood by her and walked her to the window and we looked out. "I pretended to be sick often after that, and I guess I really was . . . and my uncle was so solicitous! How I hated him!" Her teeth gritted as she spoke. "I didn't want to kill him. I wanted to destroy him, and I did . . . in a thousand ways . . . in my mind. And yet, he was always there . . . in my mind, and it was a . . . a mental block . . . with others . . . with you . . ."

"So now I know," I said softly.

"So now you know. Tell me, Donn, is there any hope for me?"

"For you, there is always hope. I wonder if there is any hope for me."

She twisted about and pressed her face close to mine. "Donn, I am not totally ignorant. I know that nature of man. I know it is one of the strongest drives. I could tell you unemotionally that behind it is God's plan for survival of the species, but one cannot be unemotional about such a drive, or urge, or force, or whatever you choose to call it. It is fundamental to life, to religion, to love . . ."

I tried to comfort her. "There is a prayer that helped me when my daughter broke her neck." My mind flicked back to another night aboard a flight over the Atlantic and a lovely stewardess.

"Say it to me," Maria whispered. "But first, turn out the light. I don't think I will again need a light burning all night. I have told you what was torturing my mind, my heart, my soul. I feel free, the bars are down . . ."

I went into the bathroom and clicked off the light, groped back to her bed and sat on the edge. Surprisingly the words came easily: "The Lord is my shepherd, I shall not want; He maketh me to lie down in green pastures, He leadeth me beside still waters. He restoreth my soul . . . Yea, though I walk through the valley of the shadow of death, I will fear no evil, for Thou art with me; Thy rod and Thy staff, they comfort me . . ."

The rest was forgotten, but she slept and I moved gently away and the world suddenly seemed a much better place. Back in my own room I fumbled through my billfold, searching for a dog-eared piece of paper which I found behind a photo of my daughter, Annette. I unfolded it and pressed at the creases and read again that most beautiful prayer written by another sinner at another time; another man with feet of clay. Somehow, I felt a kinship with King David that transcended time and events; two men who had strayed from the path of righteousness, and yet, there it was, the chance to be led back by the Shepherd. That scrap of paper was a precious keepsake. I refolded it and put it back in my wallet, turned out the light and slipped into the sheets.

It rained all day Saturday. When Sunday dawned, again with dripping skies, the four of us drove back to Rome.

Phil Barrett and I met early Monday morning at the embassy and were driven to the Italian Ministry of Defense. We were kept waiting there until ten-thirty when two generals of the Italian Army and a civilian from the ministry entered and invited us to a conference room. Compared to Friday's euphoria, there was now a decided chill in the air. I tried to conceal my worry as we went over the draft agreement in great detail: the establishment of an M-47 tank rebuild center, the purchase by the Italians of four hundred M-60 tanks, a helicopter coproduction program. And we would purchase ten million dollars worth of ammunition from an Italian firm for use in our grant-in-aid countries. There was something for everybody.

We broke for lunch and were back again at two and talked until five. Barrett was glum and taciturn during the ride back to the embassy. There we reviewed our position until seven and agreed to meet at eight the following morning. I went to the hotel, ordered a meal sent up, placed a call for Ursella in Arlington. I talked with her an hour later; she was at the hospital. She wasn't as sure as Doneva that Annette was that good; some movement, yes, but a long way to go.

We talked a bit, not saying much. And suddenly, desperately, I wanted to convey something to her. "Cella," I said, but I was inarticulate, trying to reach across thousands of miles of wire and air waves to reach my former bride.

"Yes?" she said.

"Ah, keep the faith," I said. "Kiss all the kids for me. I'll be home in a few days."

"Okay," she said. " 'bye." She sounded tired.

I went to bed that night with a strange foreboding about the Italian deal, about my family, about Goldie Flynn and about Maria; it was as if a black cloud of doom hung over us all. Was it imagination? Or a guilty conscience? Or a warning to alert me to danger?

There were long faces at the U.S. Embassy the next morning when I arrived. Barrett was not there. The head of the economics section, appearing as if he had been up all night, said that General Saragati had called Barrett about eleven the previous night, wanting to see him immediately. They met in the embassy and General Saragati presented new demands. Apparently the discussions lasted until the early hours.

Barrett showed up at noon, his face a thundercloud. He beckoned to me and we went into a small room off the ambassador's office which was debugged on a daily basis. Briefly he outlined the new demands: the U.S. must guarantee that all thirteen countries around the world would use the Italian rebuild facility to modernize their old tank fleets; the Italian firm headed by Count Agusta wanted exclusive rights to sell our helicopters anywhere in Europe and Africa. "On top of that," he added, "they want a thirteen million dollar payoff to the party before we proceed any further."

The demands were rough, but there was still hope for the deal. Later, at the Cavalerri Hilton, I joined Barrett for lunch. He had cooled down a bit and suggested I leave for the states in the morning and work on a new sales program for Morocco. He would stay in Rome a few more days to see if anything could be salvaged or if we were in for a further postponement.

"Let 'em fiddle," he said. "You and I have important things to do in the Middle East and Africa. We'll let the striped pants boys and the spooks handle the Italians for a while."

So, I went home and spent part of that fall in Arlington watching Annette slowly recover from her tumble downstairs. After nearly a month in the hospital, she came home to another three weeks in bed. For three months after bed confinement she moved about with a neck cast and a noticeable limp.

"God was watching over her," O'Malley said as our hopes grew that Annette would make a complete recovery. Maybe He was. I found myself wanting to believe that this Infinite Being, this Diety, this Stranger we only turned to during times of strife or anguish, was really concerned about one little child. I had seen so many others cruelly butchered in combat, or dying of malnutrition and disease in war-torn villages of Burma and China, or Korea, that I was skeptical and cynical about God's loving nature.

During this period, a remote part of me—the soul, perhaps, or the brain—wanted to embrace a kind, all-knowing and protective Diety; but another part—the intellect or heart—remained cold and unresponsive. And yet, a phrase from the past, perhaps from my grandmother, kept coming to mind: "Not my will, but Thine, O Lord." It didn't fit in too well with my idea of controlled destiny, and I tried to shake it out, yet it kept popping in on me, unannounced and uninvited. I continued to fight it.

Relations between Cella and me didn't really improve during this period. Added to this was still her lassitude which I did not understand. When I questioned her about the medication she was taking, she shrugged it off as a doctor's prescription to give her more energy. I didn't pursue it. Yet, I felt a growing need for Cella and I sensed she wanted me to reach out to her, but I couldn't.

The Italian deal was stalemated as fall turned to winter and winter to the spring of 1968. Phil Barrett flew to Rome every two or three months, attempting to keep the lines of communication open. Nobody turned the spigot on or off; it just continued to drip.

And Phil sent me to other countries. My traveling was intense: Ethiopia, India, Pakistan, Iran, Kuwait, Morocco, Tunisia. I worked on arms negotiations and the sale of military hardware night and day. Arms peddling became both my mistress and my master; and I was not an unwilling slave.

Chapter Thirteen

Requiem for an
Arms Peddler

IT WAS THE SUMMER of 1968 and I was back in Washington for only a day when Cella called at the office to tell me that Goldie needed to see me at his Watergate apartment as soon as possible. "He seemed very upset," she said.

Apprehension filled me as I drove to Goldie's. No telling what he was up to now that the Italian deal was in trouble. How many second mortgages was he holding on me? What was he going to ask me to do this time? But as I sped down George Washington Parkway, anger began to mix with my fear. Who in hell did he think he was just because he held a doctored tape over my head? By the time I pulled into the Watergate's guest parking area I was ready to do battle with this oversized character who thought he had a collar on me.

But a different Goldie met me at the door: his face drawn and pasty with deep lines etched in his cheeks and bags under the eyes. His voice was hoarse as he greeted me.

"Goldie," I said, "what is it, the Hong Kong flu? You smell like a hospital."

"Greta, my Swedish housekeeper, made me a mustard plaster." He managed a tired grin and opened the worn bathrobe, revealing gaudy striped pajamas and underneath the top, several layers of gauze which apparently concealed Greta's concoction.

We walked into his study and he collapsed into a leather chair. Leaning back he retrieved a glass from an end table and took a long pull on it, then winced and smacked his lips. He pointed at the glass

and said: "Hot lemon juice with a little water to cut it; stings the
fire out of my throat, but Greta says it's the only thing for whatever
I've got—flu or plain old chest cold. I've been laid up ever since I
got back. Fix yourself a drink." Goldie wiggled a slipper clad foot
in the general direction of his bar.

"No, thanks," I said, still suspicious of his motives. I wasn't about
to succumb to his enforced friendliness.

"Then ask Greta to make you a hot lemonade. She's a remarkable
woman; don't know how I managed without her."

"What's this Swedish housekeeper bit?" I probed. "You got yourself
a young, well endowed indentured servant?"

Goldie laughed and took a swig of the hot lemon juice. "Greta
may have been young at one time and she's certainly well endowed
. . . about two hundred pounds, give or take five. She's pushing 60,
just like me. Her nephew works for me in Stockholm and she has
relatives nearby in Bethesda, so I sponsored her, gave her a job as
my housekeeper; it's a good mutual arrangement."

"The best kind," I shrugged.

"Yeah, well Greta's making a special Swedish dinner for us; should
be ready in an hour. I can hurry her up if you're starving."

I shook my head. "Cella made me a Norwegian breakfast: hot cakes,
fried eggs and sausage. It can last me the whole day."

"That Cella is the best, Donn. Just as I've always said."

I eyed Goldie warily; he seemed a bit too jocular. Behind it I could
sense tension, anxiety. "What are you up to, Goldie?" I pressed. "Why
the urgency?"

"Would you believe I only wanted to see your smiling face again?"

"Sure," I said wryly. "What else?"

Goldie set down his juice, stood up and walked over to an old
fashioned, rolltop desk. From it he took out a book. Then he sauntered
back to the sofa and sat alongside me, handing me the book. I glanced
at it; Dostoevsky's *The Brothers Karamazov.*

"Have you read it?" Goldie asked.

"Way back in college."

"What do you remember about it?"

I pondered a moment. "Back then I had a spate of reading Russian
authors . . . Dostoevsky, Tolstoy, Siminov. I remember 'The Brothers'
though, because they reminded me of my uncles . . . hell-raisers, I

recall, except the younger brother who was a priest." I stared at the book reflectively. "Let's see, the father was a lecherous old man. He and one of the sons loved the same woman, a sort of prostitute. Somebody kills the father and one of the brothers is fingered and he is tried and found guilty and sent to Siberia . . . only he didn't really do it; and yet, he had this guilt complex because he had wanted to kill the old man."

"Well," Goldie said, taking back the book. "That's a fair analysis after . . . how many years?"

"Oh, twenty or so, I guess."

"I just finished it," Goldie said slowly. "An old friend of mine in Dusseldorf suggested I read it. This friend once studied for the ministry . . . Lutheran, I think . . . and he married into a very wealthy political family. He has helped me on a couple of arms deals, and yet, he's still a staunch Christian."

"Not possible to be both?" I asked, still wondering what my old adversary was up to.

"I don't know," Goldie said, and the way he said it, I knew I was about to see again the more personal side of the usually inscrutable Goldie Flynn. "Anyway," he said, laughing nervously as he tapped me on the knee with the book, "I wanted you to come over and continue the discussion I had with this friend in Dusseldorf . . . a little tête-à-tête on the immortal soul—mine."

"On second thought," I said, somewhat startled, "I think I will have a drink."

"Go ahead," Goldie said; "mix a good one. I'll stick to lemon juice right now."

As I walked over to the bar, Goldie opened the book, searching for a passage.

"*S'il n'existait pas Dieu, il faudrait l'inventer.* Do you understand that?"

Having reviewed my college French fairly recently before a trip to Morroco, I nodded. "It means that if God doesn't exist, it would be necessary to invent him."

"Right. It's the theme of a discussion between the wild Ivan Karamazov and his gentle brother, the monk, Alyosha. And, it's really Dostoevsky's theme. I think *The Brothers Karamazov* was Dostoevsky's search for God."

"And did he find Him?"

"I think he knew He existed all along, but he used the book and the Karamazov family to portray some eternal doubts, the eternal temptations; man's desire to reject God and set up his own kingdom, to build a molten calf if you will. Ah, the seven deadly sins; how we were warned as boys against them." Goldie chuckled and sipped his lemon juice.

"And how we embraced them when we became men."

"Ah, yes. I have my favorites . . . and you, Donn, you have your favorites."

I nodded, and drank from my glass and inwardly squirmed. "What attracted you to Dostoevsky?"

"During my discussion in Dusseldorf, I voiced the same doubts as Ivan Karamazov. If God exists and is all knowing and good, why does he allow so much evil to happen; not just your every day run-of-the-mill evil committed by man against his corrupted brother, but, for example, the evil against innocent children . . ."

Goldie struggled up from the recliner and began pacing the floor, obviously upset, emotion flushing his fevered face. "Donn, I'll be 60 next month; sixty years come and gone . . . where? They passed so quickly; and I've spent nearly fifty of them making money—always making money. I wanted security, I kept telling myself—a little bit for a rainy day. But, the more I got, the more I wanted; and the more it piled up, the less secure I became. I was the Grand Inquisitor."

"Not really, Goldie. I recall the Spanish Inquisition."

"Well, I'll tell you in a minute why I am like the Grand Inquisitor, but . . . the children . . ." Goldie paused and cleared his throat.

"My friend," I said, "you're ruining your voice; better wait . . . "

"No, I have to get this out of my system. It'll probably do more good than Greta's mustard plasters and lemon juice." He drained the glass and set it down. "The children . . . I never had any of my own. I love your kids, Donn; and Cella, a perfect mother . . . and the little deaf-blind boy . . . the Tadpole . . . "

I nodded, mute. In my mind, I resented the intrusion of the Tadpole on my life, even blaming him in part for the rift between my wife and me.

"Sometimes, I think of all the iron and steel we dropped in Vietnam; bombs dumped on farmer's fields and fragments tearing through thatched huts and burying themselves into the 'enemy'—the bodies of little children." He stumbled back to the recliner and plopped down.

"Steady, boy," I said. "You're sounding like a peacenik."

He shook his head and cleared his throat. "No, I've got to talk it out. Who would understand? My housekeeper? The parish priest of the church I don't go to? Maybe I could call McNamara over at the World Bank? I think now he understands. No, I need a true friend, one who's been around the horn. You know war, Donn, you know the arms business. We're friends, but, I've used you, too . . . got a couple a second mortgages out on you in fact." He laughed shakily and wiped his eyes with a pudgy paw. The tough wheeler-dealer was becoming a maudlin old man.

"Donn," he croaked, "a scotch and soda, please; easy on the scotch." I stood up and walked over to the bar and mixed a pair. I handed one to him and he took the glass and held it up: "*À votre santé.*"

"*À la vôtre,*" I said.

"You know, most of us forget we were once little kids; instead, we reject God, sneer at Christ, and make a pact with the devil. He comes along and says 'Fall down and worship me and all this is yours . . . the world and its gold and its power.' "

Goldie got to his feet again and pirouetted about the room not unlike a hippopotamus, lifting an imaginary tail in one hand. " 'Here,' the devil tells us, 'just kiss me right here . . . under the tail, just once, and all this is yours.' " He laughed and wiped his nose with a fist. "And then, having kissed the devil's tail—just once—we spend a lifetime kissing other tails . . . for favors, for special treatment, for power. 'But no,' they will tell you, 'not for power but for loyalty. Be loyal to me and all this is yours.' " He looked at me, imploringly. "Don't you see it, Donn?"

I nodded and cleared my throat. I saw it, but I really didn't want to see it.

"Look, let me tell you about children. We cannot grasp killing them by the thousands. Stalin spoke of this. 'To kill one man is murder,' he said. 'To kill a million is a statistic.' But, listen to Ivan Karamazov tell about bestiality to little children." Goldie scooped up the book and paged through it.

"Here it is . . . he is telling his brother of bestial cruelty. 'A beast can never be so cruel as a man, so artistically cruel. The tiger only tears and gnaws . . . the Turks took a pleasure in cutting the unborn child from the mother's womb and tossing babies up in the air and catching them on the points of their bayonets. Doing it before the mother's eyes was what gave zest to the amusement.' "

Goldie's voice broke and I held up a restraining hand, but he cleared his throat with great gusto and waved away my hand. "But, I was talking of little children," he continued. "Dostoevsky writes beautifully about the little children; about the well-educated, cultured gentleman and his wife who beat their own child, a girl of five. They beat her, thrashed her, kicked her for no reason. Then, they refined their cruelty—shut her up at night in the cold, outdoor privy. Can you understand why such an innocent uncomprehending creature should beat her little aching heart with her tiny fist in the icy dark and weep unresentful tears to 'dear, kind God' to protect her?"

And it was here that Goldie's voice cracked and he could not go on. Then Greta came in, saying, "Dinner is served, you betcha," and we went in to a dinner of white fish covered with a sauce, and white wine, tender steaming Swedish meatballs with bits of onion and spices in them, and glazed carrots and little potatoes. I gave Goldie the mundane happenings of the Grand Pre family which he seemed to enjoy and after the meal, we thanked Greta and went back to the study. Goldie, finding his voice, continued with his analysis.

"Donn, you may think I've gone soft-headed, but I am searching, my friend. Somehow, in this book, I have found part of an answer but also, many questions. I am fascinated by Ivan's description of the children. He uses them to teach a point. Why is the world like it is? Men are to blame, he says. 'They were given paradise, but they wanted freedom even though they knew they would become unhappy. So there is no need to pity them.' "

Goldie was up pacing again, reading: " 'I know too that some children are suffering and there is none to blame, none guilty. What comfort is it that there are none guilty? I want to see justice done—and not justice in some remote time and space, but here on earth so that I can see it myself. I want to be there when everyone suddenly understands what it has all been about. All the religions of the world are built on this longing, and I am a believer. But if all must suffer to pay for the eternal harmony, what have children to do with it, tell me, please?' "

The distraught man glanced at me then continued to read: " 'Under-stand, I am not blaspheming! I realize, of course, what an upheaval of the universe it will be when everything on heaven and earth blends in one hymn of praise and everything that lives and has lived cries aloud: "Thou art just, oh Lord, for Thy ways are revealed." But what tears me is that I can't accept the harmony and so I renounce the higher harmony altogether. It's not worth the tears of that one tortured child who prayed in that stinking outhouse to "dear, kind God!" It's not worth it, because those tears are unatoned for. They must be atoned for, or there can be no harmony. But how? How are you going to atone for them?' "

I sat there numbly not knowing what to say while Goldie paced the floor reading from the book, gesticulating, and then ad libbing. "And Ivan tells Alyosha that he cannot accept the harmony: the price is too high, he says. 'It's not God I don't accept, Alyosha, only I most respectfully return him the ticket.' And Alyosha accuses him of rebellion.

"And now . . . and now . . . " Goldie was visibly shaken, and although somewhat hoarse, regained the vigor of his voice; "Listen to Alyosha. He says, 'You said just now, is there a being in the whole world who would have the right to forgive and could forgive? But, there is a Being and He can forgive everything because He gave His innocent blood for all. You have forgotten Him, and on Him is built the edifice, and it is to Him they cry aloud, "Thou art just, oh Lord, for thy ways are revealed." ' "

Goldie sat there for a moment—it seemed an eternity—then he stood upright, beads of perspiration standing out along the furrows of his forehead. He flung the heavy book across the room where it crashed against the wall and fell to the floor in a flurry of pages. "Aaaggghh," he groaned, "for fifty years I have rejected Him and embraced the devil for power, security, money." He waved his hands and shook his massive head. "And I have ended up with nothing . . . nothing . . . "

I was speechless. His admission coupled with the quotes from Dos-toevsky painted an only too vivid picture of my own future. I too wanted the purple robes of the annointed within the sacred citadel—the Pentagon. Could I extricate myself? Did I want to? Or would I, in the end, be dashed against the rocks? Here was the proud and zesty Goldie Flynn who wheeled and dealed with the best and the brightest, humbling himself. I didn't want to humble myself.

"My friend, my friend," I said hesitantly.

"Ah, my friend . . . that's a comfort, a comfort," he croaked. Suddenly, he stood upright and threw his half-empty glass into the fireplace where it shattered with a tinkle. "God," he uttered, "how I need my spirit uplifted!"

I longed to say something reassuring to this man, but I wasn't the one; I needed the same kind of reassurance. Suddenly I saw us as two parched men dying of thirst in the desert. Goldie talked of this cool water just within reach. All we had to do was reach out— or up.

Instead I stretched and glanced at my watch: nearly eleven. "Goldie," I said slowly, "I wish you luck getting the world back to Christ. I'm skeptical. I have seen man up close and I find him basically greedy and selfish. It's hopeless to ask the church hierarchy to revert to sackcloth and ashes or the landed aristocracy to part with a portion of what has taken years of connivance and corruption to accumulate."

"I didn't say that; *you* said that," Goldie said "Look, I'm a gun runner. I'm tired of running. I know I'm greedy and selfish, but I'd like to save my own soul. You know, both Mama and Papa were devout Catholics . . . good combination, eh? Jewish Catholics." He chuckled. "Somewhere back a few centuries, my people were forced into the church in what is now Austria. But it took, and now, I'd like to get back into the fold."

"And then what? Are you going to give away all you possess and follow Jesus?" I was being too sarcastic and I knew it.

"No, but I would like to do some good. You remember one night when Ursella was talking about starting a center for deaf-blind children? Well, why don't you give up the arms peddler role and help her start such a place? I don't even know the sign language, but I could help with money. Set it up as a charity. Surround yourself with a few good people—like Ursella. Set up a center and devote ninety-three cents of every dollar to the children. Give a few kids with no chance, a chance. Maybe both of us can save our souls."

"Goldie, I'm not up to it. If people ever found out about my past, they'd slaughter me."

"People! What do you care about what people might think? Only think about what Christ might think; then, do it!"

I stood up. "Hey, Goldie, now you want to save all your friends. I'm not so sure I want it; I'm not worthy."

"Worthy! Worthy! Who's worthy? The Tadpole is worthy. None of us is worthy; that's why we need it. Donn," he said suddenly, lunging at me, grabbing my arm, "I'd like to go to confession."

I was shocked. "Goldie," I said, "I didn't bring my surplice. I can't hear your confession."

"I'm not kidding. I'm deadly serious. I've thought about it for days; it's the only way I can wash away the past and I want to start a new life, chart a different course. I know a priest over at the Blessed Sacrament Church. I'll call him. We'll both go to confession."

"Hey, count me out. I haven't been to confession in years. I'd need a week to prepare and another to tell all. Not me. I don't need it, I don't want it."

"Look, you need it, believe me. Come with me; I need some support. God, I haven't been to confession for thirty years . . . thirty years . . . " Goldie's voice trailed off and he was sweating again.

"Look, Goldie, you can't go out. You've been sick. Go to bed and say a prayer and tomorrow go to confession . . . or next week."

"No, tonight. I'll backslide if I wait. It has to be tonight."

It was tonight. Goldie called the priest and then I called Ursella and told her where we were going and she was sure I was drunk. We drove over to the Blessed Sacrament parish house and a young, heavyset priest met us at the door and we went into his study which smelled of cigar smoke and furniture polish and mahogany wood. We talked about mundane things and drank a couple cups of coffee which I knew would keep me awake the balance of the night, but it was already half over and if Goldie was actually going to confession, it probably would take the rest of the night.

Thirty years?

Then, the Father ushered me into the living room where I paged through *Time* but found myself ignoring the print and the pictures and instead looking back, examining my conscience.

It wasn't that long—maybe twenty minutes—when the door of the study opened and Goldie strode out. I had left him quivering and now he came out with a bounce and the priest's hand on his shoulder.

Father John, Goldie called him, and Father John looked at me and grinned. "Next," he said.

"No thanks," I said. "I'm just waiting for a sick friend."

Goldie looked at me, eyes bright. "I'm not sick anymore; I'm gonna live!"

After I drove Goldie back to Watergate, he invited me up for "something important." Wearily and reluctantly I followed. Then he gave me an innocent looking package no larger than a paperback novel. It was wrapped in tissue paper and secured with Scotch tape; sort of a Christmas package, I thought, without the tinsel.

"Here," he said, "some cassettes to amuse you. Only keep 'em away from Cella; she wouldn't understand. Play 'em, destroy 'em, then forget 'em. Forget I had them made and forgive me if you can. Only remember that we're friends." And then his voice grew hoarse and he cleared his throat and offered his hand: "Friends in Christ," he said.

I left and drove the short distance home in silence, my mind trying to grasp the events of an extraordinary evening. "Cassettes," he said, so I knew there was more than one tape. I patted the package in my pocket. They could have just as well been in somebody else's pocket—say Ursella's—or the secretary of defense. The thought caused my face to burn hot; not the fear of losing my job, but the thought that whoever heard them would conclude I was a stupid jerk to get caught up in such a routine game of turkey when I was the turkey.

I thought of another pocket: Goldie's hip pocket. I wonder if he thought that he still had me there. Not me, I mused, I'm still my own man. But was I? Had I ever been?

Chapter Fourteen

Showdown

I SHOULD HAVE BEEN elated at Goldie's return to his boyhood religion—return to the arms of Jesus—but I wasn't. The maudlin scene in his apartment brought out a mix of emotions in me; I was bewildered, irritated, embarrassed and uneasy. To me, Flynn was still a black-hearted rogue who would sell out his friends for a bag of gold.

I remembered the only prayer he said he ever knew—the prayer of the old Spanish gypsy: "Oh, Lord, just put me where the money is." He was an arms peddler and had made a bundle; well, I too, was an arms peddler and I hadn't made it. And yet, it was with him that I could make it. "Just leave the government and join me," Flynn had said. And now, here was the guy, who would join the devil himself to consummate a deal, wanting to cleanse his conscience. Well, if he hated himself for his greed and lust, that was his business, and if he wanted to repent, that too was his business, but to urge me to do the same was none of his business.

These thoughts preyed on my mind over the next two weeks. Flynn went back to Europe, I presumed to consummate some deals; however, I didn't have much time to dwell on his comings and goings or his efforts to seek expiation for his sins. I had troubles of my own and I was also steeped in two new negotiations involving the sale of cargo aircraft to Zaire and Morocco. I was also involved in a hot and continuing debate with the U.S. Department of State about providing Emperor Haile Selassie of Ethiopia with modern weapons. And all the time now simmering on the back burner was the most important deal of all: the Italian negotiation. Where did we stand?

Polly, Phil Barrett's secretary, called me early one morning. Phil wanted to see me immediately. I hotfooted it over to the "E" ring of the Pentagon where our lords and masters held forth.

Phil was his usual patrician self, impeccably dressed in a dark, pin stripe suit with vest. He sat at his desk as I came in, hunched forward, reading a memorandum. He didn't look up. I eased onto a brown leather davenport and picked up a copy of *Interavia.* Sometimes Phil Barrett would keep you waiting ten minutes as he worked at some particular task. Finally, he removed his Ben Franklin glasses and stared at me.

"How close were you to Flynn and Baron during the Italian negotiations?" he asked.

I felt my heart surge as I laid down the international arms magazine, and rifled through my conscience like a blackjack dealer laying out the cards. Wordlessly, I flipped up my tie and peered at the intricate designs—little squares and diamonds of pale yellow with a mottled burgundy for background. The tie, a gift from Cella, was my favorite.

I looked at Phil Barrett. "Close enough to smell the garlic," I said. "Why?"

"I think some of your friends in the army are trying to torpedo the deal in Italy; there are rumors of some collusion between private arms dealers—Flynn and Baron—and government officials. Congressman Harding is making noises about 'sin, sex and skulduggery' in Italy and other places; the Secretary has asked for an in-house investigation."

He tapped on a lined tablet with a gold pen; my heart and mind raced. "Just wanted to make sure that you and I had clean skirts. You may recall," he added in a soft voice, "I cautioned you years ago when you first joined us to be discreet."

I listened to the words, but my mind was on Flynn and his tape of the Swiss bank account offer. I had a copy hidden away in my briefcase along with the sealed packet of other tapes. *Gotta destroy them,* I thought, *but what if that damned Flynn has allowed a copy of that doctored tape to get away from him, either through carelessness or by design?*

"I remember your warning," I said. "But, what about the Italian deal? Has it come back to life?"

"It never died. I keep the pot boiling; I was with the ambassador and the new minister of defense last week, but it's still a political issue; there are certain . . . er . . . arrangements that have to be completed in that sector before we can expect to get back to our negotiations."

"Ah, the arrangements," I said, allowing myself to relax a little. "Well, the CIA station chief should be able to orchestrate something . . . the laying of the green . . . "

"You're getting to sound just like Flynn." There was a trace of a smile about the patrician face. "In fact, that may have already happened. Tostilotti was relieved as minister of defense and a new boy, a pinko, has the portfolio. He's accusing Tostilotti of taking a payoff to float the tank package."

"So, what's our worry? No deal was made." The moment I said it, I knew I was wrong. Barrett stared stonily at me, a look of mild disgust, as if to say, don't be so damned naive. But he didn't actually say it. For a minute, he didn't say anything, just studied his nails. Then he sighed, shrugged, and plucked up a manila envelope from a tray on his desk and handed it to me.

"When you finish your Moroccan negotiations next week, I want you to stop off in Rome and talk with the ambassador and the chief of the military mission. Find out what's going on. Is the Italian military still interested in getting the tank rebuild facility? Do they want the new M-60 tank? Track the political situation. I have a hunch Tostilotti will form a new government and dump the little socialist."

I was busy scribbling notes on a small pad; Phil Barrett liked for his negotiators to have small note pads when he gave instructions. "Okay, Phil," I said. I glanced at the calendar on the wrist band of my watch. "I should be in Rome by the fifteenth. Anything else?"

Phil Barrett stood up and walked toward the door. I followed. "Yes," he said. "Avoid making any contact with either Flynn or Baron. I doubt some of our able congressmen know or appreciate how business has to be conducted in the international arms biz . . . but," and here, Phil Barrett did a strange thing, for Phil Barrett anyway; he slapped me on the shoulder in an unaccustomed act of camaraderie, "good luck, Donn, both in Morocco and Italy. And . . . be discreet, understand?"

I looked him right in the eyes. "Oh, I understand." And then, trying to inject a note of confidence, I added, "Relax, Phil. We'll either score in Italy, or I'll turn in my note pads."

He laughed softly. "There may be no chance to score. I told you a long time ago, there's only so much we negotiators can do; we are only catalysts. The Italian deal is a political football. In fact, the whistle may already be blown and I'm sending you into a game that's already over. But, see what you can do."

I stood outside his office door in the hall for a moment, trying to collect myself. Not until then had the collapse of the Italian negotiations seemed possible. I left for Morocco that weekend with a strong feeling of impending doom. As the plane droned over the Atlantic, I thought of my family life: chaotic. Cella and I had had a drawn out argument the night before; Bruce had quit his summer job and was running with a group of peaceniks who were demonstrating in front of the Pentagon against the war in Vietnam; Kevin was running with his old crowd directly against my orders to stay away from that bunch of outlaws. Even Doneva, my beautiful, talented, quiet, artistic 16-year-old, was dating a long-haired, medallion-wearing hippie who would give me long discourses about the crimes we were committing in Vietnam. To top it all, his father was an Air Force general stationed just out of Saigon.

And now, Phil Barrett asking me to go back into the morass of Italy—handing me a dying turkey. And Flynn, for all his professed Christianity, his confession and supposed repentance; had he slipped somebody the doctored tape? Then I remembered I still had a copy right here in my brief case; still had the unopened packet he had just given me there too. I had thought periodically of opening the packet, but one thing or another would crop up and I would forget it. I think too, subconsciously, I really didn't want to open the packet. I knew there were additional tapes inside and I knew they would reflect indiscretion on my part which would be embarrassing and further damage an already wounded ego.

And then, as the Boeing bore through the night, it suddenly struck me that I was at odds with almost every person I knew—family, business associates, friends. For one reason or another, I was constantly rubbing others the wrong way. The realization was painful and I thrust it aside but knowing that I would soon have to deal with it.

I would soon have to deal with several things which were back there somewhere in the reaches of my mind, picking and gnawing: Maria, the very thought of her warmed me. Should I leave my shattered world and go to her? She had implied several times that this was what she wanted. It would be a good life in Madrid and at the villa in the Guadarmarma Mountains. Why not? I could work with Flynn and even tap the numbered account in Switzerland. Why not? But, despite the exciting romance, despite the idea of wealth, there was something else relentlessly probing in the back of my mind: a Calvinist conscience or the Norwegian Lutheran one of my boyhood. Goldie wasn't the only one who had memories of Mama; my own, always gentle, loving, kind, understanding . . .

"Goldie, did you ever have a mother?"

How that question had stung him. And I was startled to find out that indeed he had had a mother who was gentle, loving, kind, and understanding. I wondered what my mother would think of my shenanigans.

And I thought of my wife. How much of our separation was caused by my growing thirst for power and wealth or by my neglect of both wife and family under the guise of providing materially for them?

And what about Goldie Flynn? Despite his emotional cave-in, Goldie was no fool. He had a brilliant mind and a pragmatic shrewdness that always stood him in good stead. It was not like that old arms peddler to sink to sentimentality and pathos unless . . .

Unless what?

Unless something unusual had touched him. I shook myself and stared out the circular window of the jet liner onto a bed of pink cotton candy some five thousand feet below: majestic—cumulus bathed in the soft light of a full moon. I looked at the beauty and the grandeur and wondered. Was it possible that God could reach down and blind a man today as he had done Paul—or was it Saul—on that Syrian highway? Not that Goldie had been blinded. Maybe just shook up a bit. I would look him up in Rome, despite Phil Barrett's advice. I needed to know more about his sudden change. Or was it so sudden? I recalled several instances over the past year when he would reveal powerful, personal feelings which bordered more on mortality than business acumen. I pulled the shade over the window and dozed.

At Heathrow Airport outside London I boarded a plane the next morning for Lisbon, Portugal. As we flew over Europe I wondered if I should try to contact Maria on my stopover in Lisbon to catch the plane to Casablanca. She must be in Madrid. How long had it been since our last weekend at Civitavechia? Four months?

She was very much on my mind. I thought of the life which could be lived with Maria. But somehow, as the haunting beauty of her face floated before me, another vision seemed intermingled with it, a vision of a brown-eyed, auburn-haired Norwegian in a nurse's uniform working practically night and day to help me get through college.

Somewhere over Europe and heading south at thirty-five thousand feet and four hundred fifty knots, I thought of another journey at another time. I don't know what triggered it; perhaps a reference to James Michener's new book in the TWA magazine I had shuffled through. But I remembered one of this author's South Pacific tales in which a group of islanders sailed from Tahiti to a new island we know as Hawaii in a twin-hulled canoe, a journey twice as far as Columbus' and seven hundred years before him. For the long voyage one of the leaders, Teroro, forsook his wife, Marama, for a younger, more exciting girl, Tehani. And as Teroro bid good-by to his wife he said, "You are my wisdom, Marama; you will always be in my heart." And she had replied, "I shall pray for you."

And yet, how long was Teroro on the new island of Hawaii with the young Tehani before the excitement wore thin, the sex wore thin, and Teroro yearned for Marama, his wisdom?

In a year he went back: another hazardous sea journey of thousands of miles, back to Bara Bara and back to Marama.

And all along, one sensed that she knew he would return, for she was not only his wisdom but his strength and his fortitude.

And now I knew I wanted to make that journey back, a journey of a thousand miles and more, a journey of many months, a journey back to my wisdom, my strength, my fortitude.

Or was it too late?

As the big jet winged over the European continent, I twisted restlessly in my seat. Then I remembered the tapes and I wondered if Maria was in them. I placed the brief case on the seat table and unsnapped the cover and raised the lid. There was the recorder with its earphone jack; there was the packet.

I tore loose the wrappings. There were three casettes inside. I inserted the first tape into the recorder, plugged in the earphone and turned on the switch. The first sounds of a soft female voice jerked me upright in my seat.

It was not Maria!

Chapter Fifteen

Troubled Houses

THE FEATURED PLAYER was Billie—talking, laughing, cajoling, whispering, encouraging, sighing, weeping, moaning: a star performance. We were making the letdown for Lisbon as I finished the third tape, all featuring Miss Mason; and, of course, myself, but only as a bit player not worthy of my name being entered on the billing.

Billie Mason had sold me out to Goldie Flynn. Why? For a few moments unreasonable anger welled up within me. Not toward Goldie, because I knew him for what he was, and now accepted him for what he was, warts and all. But Billie, so in need of affection and understanding, seducing me brilliantly, selling me out to Flynn and for what? A bag of silver?

And, then, why not? After all, they were business partners in one of the world's oldest professions—arms peddling—and there never were any Robert's Rules of Order in that business.

I had expected the tapes to feature Maria Valdez. We did have some intimate conversations. And yet, I could see now that Maria was no actress. Her tapes would have been bland, something Captain Kangaroo could play to his juvenile audience without fear of The Legion of Decency.

Sadly I thought back to the days when I was strong enough and my family relations warm enough to withstand the temptations of a Maria or a Billie. These strengths had been reinforced by an inner voice, periodically cautioning: *Goldie Flynn is setting you up with Maria; treat her as a friend, nothing more.* And then Cella and I had

162

grown apart and the defenses crumbled. When Billie Mason sneaked up on me, my guard was not only down, it was out.

We landed at the Casablanca International Airport which had been built by the U.S. Army initially and later lengthened and improved by the U.S. Air Force, and still later, given as a gift to King Hassan. As we rolled to the parking area, I put away the tapes and the recorder and vowed to confront Billie when I stopped off at Rome on my way back to the States.

A staff car from the embassy met me, an Air Force colonel acting as the official reception committee. He helped me through customs and escorted me to the Tour Hassan Hotel in downtown Rabat, some thirty miles away. We had dinner together that evening and he filled me in on things political, military, and sociologic about Morocco. King Hassan wanted to upgrade his military forces and we were eager to sell him five hundred million dollars worth of planes, tanks and guns.

That evening we were gathered at a formal dinner party given by the ambassador and his lovely wife. It was late, perhaps eleven or after. We were still seated around the oval table in the dimly lit dining room, sipping after-dinner liqueurs. Wilbur Baron was also there, seated next to me. Of the eight people about the table, we were the odd couple, neither of us, for the moment, with wife or girl friend. The charming wife of the chief of the military mission was at my right and I enjoyed her chitchat, but the Baron kept interrupting with banal and garrulous comment.

I was holding my glass aloft for a refill of Napoleon brandy when the ambassador's Moroccan secretary unobtrusively approached the head of the table. I noticed a folded piece of paper pass from his hand to the ambassador's and then, the secretary slipped silently away. The ambassador studied the paper, passed it to his wife who read it after adjusting her glasses and handed it back. The ambassador then tapped lightly on the bell of his brandy snifter with a spoon. The low murmur of idle chatter ceased as if a judge had suddenly called the court to order. Even the Baron halted in midsentence.

The ambassador stood up. "My friends," he said, "I dislike injecting a note of somberness into this gathering, but I have just received some rather distressing news." He paused and glanced at the paper in his hand as if to confirm what he had read.

He looked up. "One of our guests tonight was to have been Goldie Flynn, an old friend to many of us. But business in Rome kept him away. I have received a cable from Rome telling of a plane crash in the Swiss Alps earlier this evening. It was an Al Italia jet enroute to Bonn, Germany. It is down in the Alps and a rescue team is on the way to the scene, but there is doubt if any passengers survived. My friends, I regret to inform you that Goldie Flynn was aboard that flight."

I was numb, only aware of an increase in the tempo of the chatter and the uttering of a curse on the part of Baron. I twirled my brandy snifter, trying to envision that the irrepressible Flynn was no more. Had he somehow known of his death in advance? Was this the reason for his tearful mutterings about finding his soul before it was too late? *Goldie, Goldie, what were your final thoughts?* I asked myself. Then I had the strange sensation that he had met the end with complete peace. "God rest your soul, Goldie Flynn," I murmured aloud and sipped the brandy.

And then, I was acutely aware of Baron blubbering in my ear. "Donn, I can't believe it! I can't believe it! Did he say Goldie was killed in a plane crash?"

I looked at Baron and there were tears in the big man's eyes. He looked stricken. I nodded. "Yes, at least he was in a plane that crashed and they doubt there are any survivors."

"God in heaven," the Baron muttered and I think he meant it as a prayer. "Flynn's gone out . . . like that." And he snapped his fingers. "Not Goldie Flynn!" He groaned and stuck his nose in a brandy glass, draining its contents.

At the moment, I felt more sorrow for Baron than for Flynn. I laid a hand on his arm. "Don't take it too hard," I soothed. "Goldie was as ready as any man for death. He made his peace with God a couple months ago; he even went to confession after thirty years away from the church."

Baron stared moodily into his brandy, twirling the glass by the stem. "I knew something had happened to him," he growled. "The last few months he wouldn't go for the jugular. I was afraid he was goin' soft. What came over him?"

I stared at Baron somberly. "We can survive without always going for the throat."

Baron looked at me, suddenly clear-eyed. "Not in our business," he said.

The morning paper confirmed that there had been no survivors in the jet crash and Goldie Flynn was listed among the passengers.

I flew to Rome, checked into the Excelsior and had another restless night. The following day I walked over to the offices of the Military Assistance Advisory Group, talked with the chief and later that morning he took me over to the embassy for a meeting with the ambassador. Everybody seemed to be hedging their bets. But not Gordy Rutledge, Pentagon advisor and an American businessman living in Rome. We had lunch together at the Piccalo Mundo where he filled me in on what he called "the straight scoop."

"Your Italian deal is as dead as a dodo bird," he said, as I sat in a daze, my cup of expresso untouched. He went on to relate how Tostilotti had indeed formed a new government and placed his man in as minister of defense. General Saragati had just that day been forced into retirement and a much younger general chosen as the new chief of staff. His decision, backed by the board of military experts, was that the effort to modernize worn-out M-47 tanks was useless and that the new U.S. tank, the M-60, was no good for Italian terrain. The Italians, he insisted, should opt for a coproduction arrangement with the German government for producing the German battle tank, the Leopard, in Italy.

"Our undercover people in Rome and Bonn had confirmed that the deal is for eight hundred Leopard tanks," Rutledge continued. "There will be an outright purchase of two hundred from the Germans at a unit cost of nearly three hundred thousand dollars a tank and coproduction here in Italy of six hundred more. And the cloak-and-dagger boys told the chief in Stuttgart that there was a six million dollar payoff involved."

"But why did the Italian military go for the German tank?" I asked.

"Well, in their estimation it's a better tank than the American M-60. You know, there isn't another NATO country using the M-60; the French have their AMX; the British, their Chieftain; the Krauts, their Leopard. The Leopard has several advantages: better adaptability to Italian terrain and European conditions, better size, weight, and speed. I'm afraid that the M-60, despite production improvements, is now an obsolete vehicle."

It was jolting news, but as a military man I knew it made sense. I cabled Barrett from MAAG Headquarters informing him that the Italian deal was indeed dead. Surprisingly, a weight seemed lifted from me.

I had struggled with myself about contacting Billie while in Rome. After hearing the tapes I at first wanted to confront her. Then after Flynn's death I wanted to forget her. But after the message to Barrett was dispatched, I picked up the phone and dialed her number. It rang several times, and then her musical, "Hello."

"Billie," I said. "It's Donn. I just got in. About Goldie . . . what can I say?"

"There's nothing to say," she replied. "He came into my life like an apparition, and now thirteen years later he's faded away in the same fashion. And, God help me, all I feel is a sense of relief."

I sighed audibly. "Billie, I understand."

There was a long pause at the other end. "Donn, could you come over for a short while? It's been a long time."

"A lot has happened in that time, Billie. I want to, but . . ." I hesitated, wanting to blast her about the tapes, and yet, somehow, I couldn't do it.

"But, what?"

"It'll take about a half-hour to get there."

"I'll be waiting," she said.

I rang the bell to her apartment. She opened the door with an inviting smile; a dark-haired beauty in flowing emerald green mandarin pants and matching jacket and jade pendants dangling from gold earrings. *She's had forty minutes to set the stage,* I told myself. I tried to be formal and aloof with her, but it was difficult with a woman so warm and feminine.

I called her on the tapes, but by then two drinks had come and gone and there was no longer any blast in me. What came out was a sort of childish,

"Why'd ya have to do that, Billie?"

Her answer was plain enough. "Insurance," she said.

I didn't press the issue. In business, she was as tough, cold, and pragmatic as Flynn. She had an added advantage, being a woman. And tonight, she was all woman, from the Chinese-red lacquer on her toenails to the two long, hand-carved, ivory needles emerging from both sides of a soft ball of ebony atop her queenly head.

Now she lounged decorously on a pillow-piled sofa with cigarette and a drink. I sat on the plush carpet, head lolling back against the cushions of the sofa. "There were other tapes," she said.

"I presume," I said.

"Everything you ever said in Rome is on a tape, Donn. But don't feel bad. Everything I ever said . . . almost . . . is also on tape. And for that matter, nearly everything Flynn ever said . . ." I could hear the shrug in her voice. "That's the way it is," she said; her voice was very soft.

Then she explained that when she heard of Flynn's death, she opened a certain letter he had left her in case of such an event. There was a key to a safe deposit box. In it were several tapes, stuff she'd never heard and she was furious, she admitted, about one which indicated Flynn was thinking of dropping her. But there was also a will leaving her properties and bonds, and there was the Swiss account. She was supremely wealthy and had recovered reasonably well from the tape which revealed that even she was expendable.

I went into the kitchen to refill the ice bucket, still clutching a half gallon of Johnnie Walker Red in one hand.

"Did you hear about Maria?" Billie asked.

I stopped at the threshold. "No," I said, "what about Maria?"

"She died last week, cancer of the cervix."

The jug of Johnnie Walker slipped from my fingers and crashed to the floor, splintering into a thousand pieces and splashing Scotch onto my pants legs. Billie leaped up from the sofa and rushed to the doorway. I groped for a stool and flopped on it, my legs like rubber.

Billie stood in the doorway, a shocked look on her face. "What's wrong, Donn? You're as white as a sheet!" She looked intently at me. "Were you and Maria . . . ?"

I pulled myself together. "Yes," I said. "We were close."

"When did you see her last?"

I shook my head and mumbled. "A few months ago . . . at Civitavechia."

"And she was okay then?"

I nodded. "Who told you . . . about her death?"

"Isabel sent me a cable from Madrid."

I stood up looking for a broom. Billie retrieved one from the closet, plus some towels, and we cleaned up the mess while I collected my thoughts.

"The last time we were together Maria looked so much thinner," I reflected. "The way she talked . . . the things she told me . . . almost as if she had a premonition."

"Of her death?"

"Yes, as if she were preparing for it." I was surprised to see tears streaming down Billie's cheeks as we walked back to the living room.

She leaned back on the sofa and covered her face with long, artistic fingers. Her voice was muffled. "I'm ashamed . . . for the first time in my life . . . I'm truly ashamed."

I turned and stared at her, then slowly shook my head. "That's not your style, Miss Billie. Being ashamed doesn't become you."

"No it doesn't. It's certainly not my style; and I've spent much time and money on that style. At first, I did it to please Flynn, but I found out that while it seemed to please him, it didn't make him any more attentive. I owed him a lot and I was grateful, but I could never give him the affection I so wanted to give somebody."

"You gave it to me, Billie."

She swung about and put her hand on my shoulder. "I could relate to you. I remember feeling so pleased when Goldie said to me, 'Maria won't deliver the goods and I want Donn. It's up to you, Billie.' "

"And so, the next time I was back in Rome, you snared me, eh?"

"You were not that unwilling."

It was true. I had to admit to myself that part of it was to lash back at Goldie, to take Billie from him. But in the end, I was the one taken.

"Why did you make the tapes, Billie?"

"Because he asked me to."

"Total loyalty."

"Yeah!" She stood up and paced silently on the plush carpet. "With Flynn, I was loyal . . . either you're loyal or you're not loyal."

"What about honesty?"

"Donn, you've been in Washington a lot more than I have. You must know that in politics, in government, in business, the cardinal virtue is loyalty. You can be devious and immoral, you can lie, cheat, and steal, but you don't dare be disloyal!" She inhaled deeply and let the smoke stream gently from her nostrils. "The only people I know who place honesty above loyalty are the Christians."

"Do you know any Christians?"

"A few." She smiled.

"Are you a Christian?"

"No. I've thought about it . . . at times, I would like to be, but it frightens me."

"Did you know Flynn was a Christian?"

"You've gotta be kidding. Goldie Flynn was a Jew."

"Sometimes they make the best Christians."

I told her then about my night with Flynn, about his fascination with Dostoevsky, about his confession and the return of the three tapes.

"I brought 'em back with me Billie. I meant to confront you with them, and say something clever and cutting, but . . . I could never think of anything particularly clever or cutting." I reached inside my coat and extracted the three tapes and tossed them on the cocktail table. "Here," I said, "the story of my life."

She stared at them, and then, with a sweeping motion of a leg, sent them flying across the room. "We can erase them," she said.

"But not the memories. Keep 'em and play 'em after I'm gone, Billie."

"Donn," she whispered, clutching my arm. "Stay a few days. Let's forget the tapes—there's no more reason for tapes. Stay and we'll make some new memories."

I eased her gently away and stood up. "Thanks, Billie. I hope we'll still be friends."

"Donn, where are you going?"

"Home, back to domesticity."

"Just like that."

"Just like that. I need to grow up, Billie. Once you accused me of knowing everything but myself. It was a sad indictment, but true. It's taken me a long time to see it." I moved to the door leading to the hallway and placed one hand on the knob.

"Donn, don't just walk out." She was struggling for expression as the glib, flip style was gone. "I'm not what you think . . ."

"No, you're not; and neither was Maria, and neither was Goldie, and neither am I. I'm not what you think."

"Well, then for God's sake, what are you?" Her face was drawn in anger and the hazel eyes flashed fire. "Don't you know? Well, I know what you are! You . . . you're no better than I am, no better than Goldie; you're the same, the same . . ."

I left her then. My last image was of her standing there in the emerald green Mandarin pants and matching jacket, a twisted look of pain and anguish on the beautiful face. Billie now had material wealth beyond measure, and yet, she had never seemed so lonely, so lost.

And I was just as lost. The plane trip back to Washington was one of torment. Death was all about me: Goldie, Maria, the Italian deal. My family situation was in disarray. As the plane droned across the Atlantic heading west with the sun, other images unfolded in my mind: of Ursella, the mother of my children, six kids of varying ages growing up and away—my biggest responsibility and my greatest failure. Was it possible to salvage any of what I had let slip away?

My oldest son, Bruce, met me at Dulles Airport. Bruce, who was supposed to be in his second year at North Dakota State. He was silent and moody loading my luggage into the station wagon.

"School out early?" I asked.

"No, dropped out," he said.

"Couldn't cut the mustard?"

"Didn't see the point."

"So, what are you gonna do?"

He shrugged, saying nothing as he drove the wagon onto the expressway heading toward home. I was irritated, not only at the silence, but at the long, blond hair and the peace medallion hanging from a leather thong about his neck: marks of independence. And yet, this was my studious son who, it seemed like just last week, had a crew cut and wore conservative clothes.

"How's our Annette?" I asked.

"Great. I think she was elected captain of an all boys' football team."

"That's our tomboy!" At least something good, I thought gratefully; she had recovered fully from the tumble downstairs.

"And Doneva?"

"Okay. I taught her and Colin to play guitar."

"And how are they doing in school?"

"Doneva's straight A; Colin's holdin' his own, thinks he's a jock."

"Bully for Colin. Any more good news?"

"Yeah, Kevin dropped out of school and went to Florida with some girl in a Lincoln Continental."

"Well," I said flippantly, "I'm glad she has a Lincoln Continental." But my chest was tight and I thought of Father O'Malley saying, "How like you they are, Donn." True, I thought, true.

Bruce drove on in moody silence, swinging off the parkway and onto Dolly Madison Boulevard. Suddenly, he said, "Tad can hear, Pop."

I was startled. "How do you know?"

"I was playing my guitar the other night and he was stumbling around the rec room; he touched the amp and stood there bouncing up and down."

"Just feeling the vibrations?"

"No, I swear he was hearing. I hooked up earphones and clamped them onto his amplifier." He looked over at me. "You haven't seen his new hearing aids, have you?"

"No, your mother mentioned he was getting them when I called home the other night."

"Well, he wears this harness, see? It has batteries and an amp built into a little leather box on his chest and cords run to his ears."

"And they work?"

"Yeah, really great. I hooked the earphones to him and played different things. He sits real still on a slow piece, but bounces like crazy on the rock stuff."

"Well," I said. "I'm proud of you. You're really looking after the Tadpole."

"Maybe I can teach him to talk . . . with the amps and stuff."

"Maybe you can. Why don't you set it up as a winter project? Maybe you need a year off from academics."

"It wasn't the studying I minded, Pop. I . . . I just didn't seem to fit in up there. You're either a cool guy or a jock or a hell-raiser, and I'm not any of those."

"You don't have to run with a pack."

"Nah, I guess not. Sometimes, I think I'm a little queer . . ." He looked quickly at me and laughed, embarrassed. "Not that way, Pop. But you know, odd. Sometimes I wonder if I'm losin' my marbles."

"We all do . . . I have occasional doubts about my sanity and the reality of things. Don't sweat it . . . it's normal. You don't have to probe into theology to appreciate religion and be concerned about the starving people in India to appreciate life."

"You're preachin' again, Pop."

"Yeah, I guess I am. I preach too much and act too little. You'll find, Bruce, that much of life is form rather than substance. It makes being a hypocrite a little more palatable. You're a loner, Bruce, which is all right. It takes courage for a man to live with his thoughts and develop his own beliefs."

"Aaaaaaaaamen!" Bruce expertly swung the wagon into our cul-de-sac on Tazewell Street and into the sloping driveway.

It was a week later when Kevin returned from Florida. He'd been drafted.

By that time, Bruce had left for Boston. We weren't to get a report about his doings there until Christmas when we learned that Bruce and a friend of his from a wealthy family in Upper Saddle River, New Jersey were living in a garret in a slum and working in a warehouse. Most of their meager earnings was going to an elderly widow who lived in the same slum and who was supporting a useless brother ill with emphysema. Oh, noble Bruce and your search for altruism, I thought.

When will you grasp reality?

Kevin went to the barber's and had his long corn yellow mane sheared off and done up in ten packets, each tied with a red ribbon. He presented them to ten different girls, one being his mother. Late that evening, he came into my study and handed me a cigar box. I raised the cover and peered inside.

"What are all the goodies, Kev?"

"Grass, mostly."

"Grass?"

"Yeah, you know, maryjane . . . marijuana. Bruce 'n' me tried some at a party."

"Use much of it, Kev?"

"Nah, not really; don't like bein' a part of the crowd."

"And this stuff here?"

"That's cough medicine; terpenhydrate; has codeine in it; for guys who can't stomach beer or booze. It'll get you high."

"Quite a collection. What are you going to do with it?"

"Give it to you," he said. "Thought we'd better straighten ourselves out before you . . . ah . . . before you beat the crap out of us." He edged toward the door.

"Where are you going, Kev?"

"Thought I'd better get some more boxing lessons. Lemme know if you wanna go runnin' again, Pop."

"Okay, Kev; how about tomorrow evening?" He nodded. "And, Kev . . ."

"Yeah, Pop?"

"Thanks."

Kevin left the next week for the army.

Chapter Sixteen

The Last Big Deal

So, I CAME BACK home and spent a quiet week with remnants of my family, trying to pull it back together again, reaching out for my wife in a sense, but too proud or too stubborn to be effective.

There was one moment in which we found ourselves together. On a rambling drive in the country we came across a piece of farmland for sale. It hadn't been worked for years and what was left of the house was crumbling. Even so, there was something about the place that touched us. On checking with the local realtor, I found it could be had at a low price with a very small down payment.

Obviously it was a place that we wouldn't use for years, but I made a ridiculous offer anyway and then was surprised to find it accepted.

Except for convincing Annette that it would be a long time before she could keep a horse there, I had almost forgotten the farm the following Monday when I returned to the office. By then, sorting out details of the Moroccan negotiations occupied my mind. It was only 8:00 A.M. and officially the work day didn't begin until 8:30 A.M. but Phil Barrett summoned me.

I hurried obediently to his plush office, found him seated at his huge mahogany desk, silent, except for a nervous drumming of fingers on the plate glass top. There was a look of pain etched on his finely chisled countenance and it startled me. We had been led to believe that the Boston Brahmins were made of cold steel, incapable of showing warmth or emotion.

174

We chatted aimlessly and half-heartedly about Morocco and Italy. Then, he came away from his desk and sat next to me on the brown leather davenport.

"Tough about ol' Goldie," he said.

"Yeah," I replied, "tough."

Phil Barrett reached next to him for a silver carafe of coffee and poured two cups into his delicate Spode china. "Help yourself to cream or sugar," he said, handing me a cup and saucer.

"Thanks, I'll take it black."

"Have you heard about the Baron?"

"What about him?" I said, slightly uneasy. "I saw him in Morocco; had dinner with him at the ambassador's residence."

"He died of a heart attack in a restaurant in Rabat; went just like that." I watched as Barrett snapped his fingers. "The ambassador is having the remains shipped here. Funeral's tomorrow. I think you and I should go. He had no relatives back here as far as I could determine."

"Sure," I said, my mind gone cold. I sipped the hot, black coffee, hoping its warmth would go further than my stomach.

"Funeral's set for ten thirty at the National Presbyterian Church on Nebraska Avenue. We can drive over in a staff car."

I nodded, staring into the depths of the coffee cup, seeing nothing but a void, a beckoning darkness.

Phil Barrett leaned forward, balancing the cup and saucer in his skeletal hands. "Nothing any of us can do for the Baron, Donn. He's gone to his reward . . . which we all must do. Have you ever pondered that one, Donn?" He paused and sipped his coffee.

"No need to answer." He smiled wanly and waved the thought away with an artistic hand. "May God have mercy on his soul." And then, Phil Barrett, a confirmed Irish iconoclast, I assumed, made the sign of the cross.

"Amen," I said, rather fervently, wondering whether Phil Barrett was in fact Irish or Catholic.

A week later Barrett called all his lieutenants into his office and made a short announcement. He had resigned from the government to become head of the political science department at a large and prestigious university. Phil's urbanity and incisiveness had returned. He gave us a crisp summary of the arms negotiations throughout the world, assured us that our jobs were secure and stated that his replacement would be announced shortly: a prominent executive pulled away from the military-industrial complex.

Barrett loved class. He went out in style to accept a classy position.

Later I asked Dave Chambers about the behind-the-scenes events. Dave didn't see any direct connection between Barrett's resignation and the collapse of the Italian deal. But he said that someone in the civilian hierarchy of the Pentagon had apparently used a four-star army general, who had been Dave's regimental commander in Korea, to buy twenty million dollars' worth of Italian ammunition, even though the general had just issued a policy statement to the effect that ammunition production in the United States was sufficient to meet all contingencies. The army was also concerned that the spare parts arrangement for tanks would not only give the Italians a worldwide monopoly but would also give them a slice of U.S. military requirements for tank parts.

At the same time the army staff was upset by what it perceived to be a threat to its logistical role. A memo sent to the secretary of defense from the secretary of the army said in part that the army had concluded that Italy was no longer interested in taking over world-wide support of M-47 tanks, that they would continue to look to the U.S. Army to support their M-47 tank fleet with spares and diesel engines. Therefore, the U.S. Army was prepared to continue worldwide support of all M-47 tanks and would enter into separate agreements with any country desiring to modernize its tank fleet. So the army secretary advised that further tank negotiations with Italy on the matter be terminated.

"And did the secretary of defense agree?" I asked Dave.

"Sure, what else could he do? The cards were all stacked against the program."

"We were beating a dead horse," I murmured.

"No, you had a mission and you pushed for its success. You can't do more than that. Sometimes there are overriding political or military reasons."

"But I still don't see why this brought on all the flak."

Dave shrugged. "Apparently the secretary of defense had a copy of an incriminating memo from Wilbur Baron to Phil Barrett showing how the Italian pot would be split: so much to the Americans, so much to the Italians. Baron was to get two thousand dollars per rebuilt tank and from his cut he was to give a high government official five hundred dollars a tank."

Dave stared at me somberly. "There was no proof that the official had agreed to this arrangement, nor that he was using his position as a government negotiator to influence the deal. The proposal could have been Baron's idea alone, but it evidently generated enough heat to give Baron a fatal heart attack and convince the official to resign."

I wondered to myself if Barrett's decision to resign was coincidental.

"It's a dirty business, isn't it, Dave?" I said wearily.

"It doesn't have to be."

I shook my head. "I'm afraid it always will be."

The weeks passed and my work settled down to familiar patterns again, but the zest I had had for the international arms game was gone. I no longer looked forward to the trips, the negotiations, the excitement of new places and new things. Whether it was the corruption, the deaths of Maria, Goldie and Baron, my floundering marriage, or Phil Barrett deciding to quit, or a combination of these things, the business had become sour in my mouth.

Which helps to explain why Sean O'Malley's telephone call to my Pentagon office that October day was so welcome. It had been several months since our last contact. I invited him over for dinner that evening.

He drove up about seven thirty in a tan Oldsmobile Toronado, and Colin and Annette ran down the driveway to greet him. He clutched them about the shoulders, then kissed Cella and pulled us all close. "It's sure good to come home," he said.

And then we were inside clustered about the Tadpole. He was printing assorted words in large block letters with a crayon and making signs for the words with his hands. O'Malley was amazed. He refused my offer of a drink and remarked that he hadn't had one for months. "I'm getting away from the old army habits," he said.

Dinner was enjoyable, filled with reminiscences. And after the meal, Colin and Doneva produced their guitars and sang *Fire and Rain* and *Country Roads* and *Pretty Pamela Brown,* and then we all sang *This Land Is Your Land,* Sean sprawled in a chair, booming out a rich baritone. Then, Colin made a fire in the fireplace and he and Annette went to their rooms to do homework. The Tadpole went to bed. Cella and I and Sean drifted into the rec room where he waved away another offer for a drink and offered me a cigar instead. We puffed contentedly as he explained how he had always wanted to be a priest in a small town and work with teenagers. "I love the military, Gramps, but there was always this tuggin' at the heartstrings to become a part of a community, to grow roots. I'll be retirin' next month," he said.

It had been another long day for Cella, and by ten thirty she was nearly dozing. We sent her off to bed and I turned on the TV. The news report detailed the kidnapping of a world figure, the bombing of a New York office building, and the conviction of a public official for corruption.

The editorial comment after the news ended with the statement: "Something has gone wrong in our society."

Sean sat on the edge of a recliner, a study in perplexity. "I agree," he said. "Something has gone wrong . . . but what?"

"Nothing wrong with the society, Sean, only with some of the people who live in it."

"Maybe I'm finally emerging from my cocoon, Donn, after leaving Ireland. I became an American citizen almost thirty-six years ago and lived in the army for most of that. Sure, we saw some violence, but it was expected in a war. Now, we live in perpetual violence where organized crime and street crime and homicides and rapes and burglaries are the highest in the world. We live in a nation whose Capital has streets that are not safe after sundown. We live in a nation where the ripoff and the payoff and the kickback are the accepted ways of doing business. It's not only in the international arms business; it's in the state capitol, city hall, the auto repair shop, lawyers' offices and funeral parlors. *Caveat emptor* is our motto."

"And the golden calf is our god," I muttered.

"Some people think it happened overnight," O'Malley said. "It's been goin' on as long as I've been here; the new society built on the twin pillars of the welfare state and the warfare state. And manipulating politicians try to bring about a utopia."

"It'll never happen," I said. "The more you get, the more you want. We start simply enough, wanting only an extra suit, then a car, and a house too; and then, another car, and then a beach house and maybe an airplane to get from here to there: never enough. So you slip a little, swing a deal, get a little money on the side; just enough to cover a mortgage payment, maybe. Once you slip, it's easy to slip again . . . and again . . ."

"And you've slipped?"

For a moment I stared at the floor. I had slipped in so many ways. I looked up at Father O'Malley.

"Yes I have, Father. You warned me and yet, your gratuitous advice went unheeded. On top of that, I've neglected my family and we've drifted apart, Cella and I."

O'Malley rose from a chair, strode over and placed a hand on my shoulder. "Donn, now that Cella's fought the cancer battle and won, the two of you have a lot of good years to share."

The glass slipped from my fingers and fell with a faint thud on the carpet. I stooped to recover the tumbler and three ice cubes, my mind in a daze. "Cancer battle . . ." I mumbled.

Father O'Malley clutched my arm. "You mean . . . after all these months you never knew your own wife had cancer of the thyroid? You let her fight that battle all alone?"

Dumbly, I nodded, conscious of the accusation in his voice but unable to grasp the full import of what he was saying.

"Great God in heaven!" he roared. "I remember her tellin' me almost two years ago when I was first stationed at the Pentagon. She told me then not to tell you and I didn't; I assumed she'd tell you in her own good time." He shook the craggy head. "But didn't you sense something wrong?"

"Yes," I groaned. "Yes, I can recall the medications and her trips to the doctor; low blood sugar, she said, and lack of iron in the blood. I was too self-centered, too much concerned about where I was going. We drifted and I assumed she'd lost interest in me. She had her life and I had mine . . ." I stood peering but unseeing into the flickering flames.

O'Malley gripped my shoulder and leaned against the mantlepiece looking at a picture above the mantle.

"One of Cella's paintings?" he asked.

"Right," I said. "It's an old barn on a dilapidated farm down in central Virginia; Cella and I fell in love with the place and bought it months ago. I've hardly had a chance to even see it, but someday I'm gonna retire down there, raise cattle and horses."

"Why not now, Gramps?" O'Malley snuffed out the cigar in an ashtray on the mantlepiece.

I laughed shakily. "No guts, Sean. Afraid to cut the umbilical to the government trough."

"You can't do it alone, man."

"Alone?"

"Yeah. It takes two for that kind of courage. No, I'm wrong; it takes three."

There he was, talking about "three" again.

"You're speaking in riddles, O'Malley."

"Let me unravel it a bit," he answered. "I'm leaving for retirement shortly, cutting my own umbilical from my second mother, the U.S. Army. It's a new venture. Alone, I couldn't hack it. But I'm getting a special kind of courage from an old friend I've talked to over the years."

"Who? General Sampson?"

"No, not Frank Sampson, though we're good friends."

"Well, *who?*" I persisted.

"Jesus Christ."

"Oh."

"He is the one I've been trying to tell you about, Donn. A good marriage calls for a commitment by husband and wife to Jesus. I know Cella has made it, but I wonder about you."

"Oh, c'mon, Sean . . ." I began, but Father O'Malley held up his hand.

"A philosopher I've read, Donald T. Kauffman, says it better than I can, Donn. *A good marriage is not a contract between two persons but a sacred covenant between three. Too often Christ is never invited to the wedding and finds no room in the house.*"

He looked at me for a moment. "Invite Him in, Gramps, invite Him in."

We walked down the driveway in silence, clasped each other warmly and O'Malley climbed into the tan Oldsmobile and turned the key. As the engine roared, he extended a hand out the window. "Ask for courage; He'll give it to you in abundance. Ask for fortitude; He'll give it to you. Ask for the true bonds of holy matrimony, an affectionate wife and a warm bed; you'll get them, Lad. But, it works both ways. He wants something in return. He wants you to obey Him and keep His commandments; that's all—a fair exchange. God bless you, Donn; my love to Cel' and the kids."

He backed out of the drive, waved, and the big car purred out of the cul-de-sac onto the main road. I stood there awhile at peace; the night was cool and pleasant. I yearned suddenly for the Dakota cornfields in the fall and a pheasant hunt with my dad and brother. Then I sighed and walked back into the house, back to the rec room where I retrieved my glass from the mantlepiece and threw another oak log on the fire. I edged a chair close and studied Cella's painting in the flickering light and pondered O'Malley's words and the sad condition of our society and my life.

Over the years, I mused, I had come to believe in a stated axiom of my grizzled first sergeant in Korea: *Get the other guy before he gets you.*

Over the years, I was an interested spectator in Washington, D.C. as the meanest and toughest and biggest of the old bulls sparred in the arena. I watched from the peanut gallery as old bulls like LBJ took on and gored former friends and colleagues. Goldie had summed it up: "Always go for the jugular."

Yet Goldie had waffled at the end. Too much blood? Am I about to do the same?

Inside I yearned for the peaceful pastures, the green and pleasant valley with a trickling stream, rock-bottomed and flowing with trout, each with but one mission—to cast himself on my hook . . .

The shadows of senility?

Maybe. I was awakening at three thirty some mornings and wandering about the house, or eating a bowl of cold cereal saturated in skim milk in the confines of the kitchen, hearing ghosts, whispers of recrimination, self-doubt cropping up more often—too often. The Washington pit is no place for a bull with self-doubts, especially one with blunted horns.

But not yet a steer . . . not yet.

I'll leave when the time is right. Would I be missed? Does pulling your fist from a pail of water leave a hole?

What had I accomplished? In deference to the really big bulls, I was never very often in the ring; usually only after the crowd had departed would I enter—with short-handled broom and broad-bottomed shovel, to sweep a bit, and perhaps to retrieve a rose, and to reflect a bit as I sniffed that faded rose . . .

The fire had burned low; only an occasional flame flickered from the glowing embers.

Had I, like Ferdinand, lost my intestinal fortitude for the fight? Or . . . ? It was a question that had been building within me longer than I had realized. Was I completely fed up with the arms business?

I stared into the dull red remnant of the log.

My work had become so all-consuming that I had to learn from a friend that my wife had fought a two-year battle with cancer. A deep sadness filled me. The one I had promised God to love, cherish and honor had to face it alone while I dallied in Europe, indulging myself in a twisted concept of romantic fulfillment.

How easy it was to understand how men like me could drift from the principles of morality and ethics into something called political expediency.

Stirring the embers with a poker, I grimaced. It took a shock, it seemed, to bring me back to reality. And the shocks lately had been many. Even Phil Barrett's unexpected departure to the educational field had shaken me.

I leaned back and tried to picture Phil as a professor. I wondered if he'd tell his young students what the arms business was really like. Would he get past the academic fact that until men halt their hatred and deception, their enslavement and murder of their fellowmen, that the world will continue to depend upon weapons for defense?

Would he tell them that producing arms has become such an overshadowing part of our life that one quarter of our nation's work force is now either directly involved in or closely allied in building the machinery of death?

Of course, he could logically point out that our overseas arms sales help bolster our critical balance of payments, help offset all that incoming oil and the VWs and the Sony television sets and Nikon cameras, the Gucci loafers and the French wines.

And Phil might even tell them about the economic theory of John Maynard Keynes which we arms peddlers practiced as truth: that no other business is so cyclic in nature. Munitions and weapons along with their ground and air transports become obsolete; they wear out or blow up and burn up in man's ancient pursuit of destroying his fellowman. So there's never a danger of producing too much; it's all waste and the faster you consume it, the more production runs you can make that will equate with profits, jobs and prosperity.

But will you tell them the rest of the story, Phil? I wondered. *Will you tell them about the arming of petty tyrants the world over so they'll jump when their chains are jerked?*

How about peddling weaponry to both sides, and even providing them with the funds, like the little Jordanian king of the Hashemites? Both the state department and the CIA poured millions a year into his pocket and we, the defense department, armed him to the teeth. At the same time we did the same for his cousins across the Jordan River. And Congress, in its wisdom, will either forgive the consequent debts or we'll extend credit to them for twenty years at three percent.

Will you tell them that, Phil?

I thought about other leaders who consider their small countries personal fiefdoms and selectively strip them, tucking a little away in Switzerland or France and buy up farmland in the United States in case they have to leave.

Gangsterism? Sure, maybe Phil will tell them that payoffs flourish in organized crime and corrupted unions, just as they do in international arms sales. The bagmen and wheeler-dealers rake it in on every transaction and second mortgages proliferate to keep all the sheep in flock.

Will you tell them all about it, Phil? I leaned forward to stir the fire again and grimaced. No, he wouldn't. For he'd have to tell the rest of the story. And that part was something none of us cared to think about. But I could not escape it now, the ultimate end of our dealings. I sank back in the chair as visions swirled before me.

I saw American mothers and fathers working in a Pennsylvania factory assembling fuses for cluster bombs; just ordinary people doing their jobs. We peddlers sold them to a mideastern country; just doing our jobs. A few years later good mothers, fathers and children in southern Lebanon are shredded into fragments by the same bombs dropped by pilots; just doing their jobs.

I covered my face with my hands. But the black visions of death persisted. I saw sixty Ethiopian cabinet ministers and other highly educated officials pulled out of their dank prison cells one cold gray morning. Some were friends of mine—men I had dealt with. They were lined against a stone wall. There, young officers who had wrested control of the government gave a signal in the name of the "Provisional Military Administrative Council."

Four air-cooled, lightweight M-60 machine guns filled the prison yard with a roar and the wall behind the men blossomed bright red.

I remembered our sales pitch on these guns: *"An effective tool, fires a cyclic rate of seven hundred fifty rounds of steel-jacketed slugs per minute."*

The older men, some cut in half, slumped to the ground which ran with blood.

"If the maintenance is good, these guns seldom jam."

All that was left of educations in the French Lycee, the Sorbonne and the École des Haute Études in Paris were red-gray brain fragments plastered to the wall.

"The guns cost $4,500 each in units of less than twenty. However, in quantities of one hundred or more, we can offer a highly favorable price of only $3,850 each."

A sickness welled within me. It would happen again and again. Educated, patriotic men in Morocco, Zaire, Jordan, Iran and other countries would be lying on cold slabs, their bodies laced with bullet holes.

Death and destruction were the ultimate products of our work. I sank back in the chair. And amid the quietness of a sleeping house, a deep certainty filled me.

I knew I no longer wanted to be a part of the arms business. I could no longer condone it or be involved in it. I would leave it and leave the government. Phil Barrett might give me that cool smile and say, "Don't tell me that you've weakened, Donn, and become susceptible to the booze, broad and bread temptations?"

But I knew the reason went far deeper than that. I had seen what the new morality was doing to my children and family life and to other families and it was not good.

I could sit back and prate about declining standards of conduct, drugs and alcohol in the schools, and corruption of our institutions. But it would all be hypocrisy unless I gave up my individual role in the corruption of that society.

Somewhere along the line I had subscribed to the philosophy of the supremacy of the state and to the deviousness and opportunism of Metternich and Machiavelli. Had it cost me my immortal soul?

Sitting in my easy chair with an untouched drink beside me, the way seemed clear. If I wanted to save that soul and my family and restore tranquility to my life, I would have to turn to the One whose teachings were disharmonious with arms peddling. I could not serve both masters.

So that evening I reached a final decision. It was not through analytical reasoning but the culmination of a continuing struggle between the material and the spiritual. I remembered the two friends who had won it all materially and yet opted for the spiritual at the eleventh hour.

Had I, too, reached the eleventh hour?

I stood and stretched and flung the untouched Scotch onto the glowing coals.

Suddenly I wanted to see Cella very much.

Chapter Seventeen

Encounter on
the Towpath

I PEERED INTO THE bedroom. The light was out, but I had a feeling she was awake.

"Cella?"

"Yes?"

I turned on the light and said in a voice choking with emotion; "Why in the name of God did you never tell me?"

"Tell you what?" she asked.

"That you had cancer of the thyroid."

She sat up in bed, looking like one of my daughters. She sighed a bit sheepishly. "I wanted to fight that one myself," she said.

"But, why?" I persisted.

"I . . . I didn't want your pity or your sympathy, I just wanted your love . . . I . . . was afraid you would do something drastic like quit your job and stay at home and take care of me. I knew how much the job meant to you . . . I didn't want to interfere."

"Ursella, we could have worked it out."

She looked up at me, hurt in her eyes. "Could we?" she asked.

"But, you . . . you seemed so cold and distant," I said. "If you wanted my love, why didn't you bend a little to . . . to make yourself lovable?"

"I wanted to win the fight against the cancer . . . and Doctor Ryan has told me I've won; but in case I lost, I . . . didn't want the loss to be that much of a loss to you . . ." She broke then and I should have gathered her up. But there had been so many months

186

of coldness and I was torn up inside myself. Suddenly, I was flooded with emotion I was afraid I couldn't control. "I'm going for a run," I said.

As I headed for the door she called, "Daddy." She hadn't called me that in years. When I turned, she smiled and added, "Have a good run." I nodded slowly, turned off the light and went to the den and rummaged for a warm-up suit and tennis shoes.

As I pulled on the suit, I was acutely conscious of how much it had shrunk since I last put it on months before. I had to sit on the bed to tie my shoes and my belly got in the way. Outside Duke John, a Samoyed husky, Annette's birthday gift the previous year after her recovery from the fall down the stairs, joined me. As I shuffled along through Chain Bridge Forest with Duke John, all the collected memories tagged alongside, the good and the not-so-good. What happened, I wondered? What happened to duty-honor-country? What happened to a once solid marriage and the close family ties? Where are all my children tonight? What pulled me away from them?

I shuffled on, down the steep hill leading to Chain Bridge and onto the bridge and then down the iron steps to the towpath where, winded, I walked and wondered. Duke John skittered off the trail and I was alone with a brilliant moon flickering through the skeletal trees of a cold, clear and still night. Myriad stars were out, winking above and in the blackness of the canal. I shuffled along again, carrying two hundred pounds on a frame built for one hundred seventy-five and my heart was proportionately heavy.

I broke into a trot and ran past Lock 7 on the canal, up the little incline, and Duke John was with me again, padding softly alongside, tongue lolling out, enjoying the night and the run. He was not burdened with either a fat belly or computerized conscience, loving, not questioning what God through nature had seen fit to give him: health and stamina and an affectionate heart.

I, too, had received ample portions of the same. What happened to them? Who had robbed me of those most precious possessions— faith in God and love of country? Where had they gone? And again, I heard Goldie saying . . . so long ago, but like yesterday . . . "Oh, I traded mine in on something called business acumen." How clever. How true.

Was Goldie corrupt? I wondered. He was or he wouldn't have

sought repentence. What about Grand Pre . . . me . . . corrupt? Yes or no? If yes, who could have done it to me? Goldie? But then, another set of words from Taylor Caldwell's *Captains and the Kings* sprang out of my memory: "No man corrupts another; he corrupts only himself and therefore, he should not plead for compassion."

But, I don't want compassion. I am still too tough for compassion. I don't want it, I don't need it . . . and yet . . . how I need it . . . help . . . compassion . . . an uplifting of my spirit.

I stopped again, winded, and leaned against a giant maple alongside the trail, its mighty branches jutting over the canal. *Ahhh, the fruit of the vine and all those rare steaks and prime roasts. How they caused the blood to beat through these tired arteries!* I could feel the pressure like a rubber band tight around the head. I remembered how Kevin and I not that long before had raced down this same trail, Kevin out ahead like a young colt kicking up his heels, showing off. And I was proud of him too. He could beat me hands down, but then I could keep up. What happened? Kevin, laddy, we drifted apart.

Should I have showed him more compassion . . . humbled myself a little? I always had to be right and Kevin was wrong . . . and Bruce was wrong, too, to drop out of college. But could *I* have been wrong? Do other guys ever admit to being wrong? If I was ever wrong, I could always rationalize it. There was always a good reason. Several in fact.

But tonight, under the scrutiny of a full moon on a clear and cold and awfully late night, the reasons didn't wash. I could no longer kid myself. I had been wrong.

It hit me suddenly that this was the spot, here where I was standing, where Ursella and I had brought the kids for picnics. Right here by the maple we had built charcoal fires and roasted hot dogs and marshmallows. Here on this very tree hung that old vine, and the kids would grasp the vine, and I would give them a mighty shove, and they would sail up and out and over the canal and squeal in pretended fright and, loving it, ask for more. As I remembered, I was suddenly conscious of that vine, ageless, timeless, buffeting against my shoulder as a light breeze sprang up, much like the tapping of a friendly hand.

I grasped at it like the drowning man grasping for a reed and all the happy memories came flooding back, washing over me in peals of laughter of happy children at play and a loving wife beside me,

the kids running out ahead, and Cella and I striding behind like shep-
herds hand-in-hand, or swinging a toddler between us, grasping pudgy
hands and swinging the child up, fat, little legs tucked in glee: once
Colin, replaced by Annette, replaced by the Tadpole. And we would
recite bits of old fashioned poetry—corny stuff from long-gone gram-
mar school days, while swinging a toddler in cadence:

> How do you like to go UP in a swing,
>   Up in the air so blue?
> Oh, I do think it the pleasantest thing
>   Ever a child can do.

And then, I was no longer holding onto the vine . . . but was on
my knees alongside the towering maple, gasping from a terrible, aching
pain at the base of my skull and between my temples, like gigantic
hands crushing, like a pair of powerful arms about my chest squeezing,
squeezing. I lost all track of time, whether a minute or an hour, I
don't remember. The maple tree became my Uncle Carl crushing me
in his sinewy arms and then tossing me high over his head. Then it
was my Grampa Fatty and I was angry at him for hurting my grandmother's feelings. . . .

*I am five again and I can see the hurt in her eyes at the breakfast
table as my grandfather takes his plate, heavy bone china with little
dots of blue around the edge—little bluebells, my grandmother called
them as she lovingly dried each piece with a bit of sacking—and Grandpa
Fatty hurls the plate and the two eggs on it to the floor where it smashes
into many pieces. As the yellow yolk runs onto the floor and the gray
cat dashes from behind the stove to lick it up, my grandmother stands
there, gently, rubbing her arthritic hands in her apron, saying nothing,
but looking at my grandfather with a look of hurt in her eyes. "I
don't like raw eggs," he says. I get up from the table and beat at
him with my fists and kick his shin. Grandpa Fatty calms me down,
puts on his battered hat, gets a dust pan and broom and cleans up
the bits of broken plate. Later grandmother hugs me close. . . .*

I beat against the tree with my fists and the dam burst inside me.
I heard myself make animal noises that frightened Duke John. I heard
his whines and I felt his tongue licking wet cheeks; and as I beat
against the tree, I prayed . . . *God help me . . . God help me.*

And then, the thought: *I am having a heart attack!*

I leaned my forehead against the gnarled tree, feeling the bark biting into my forehead and I talked to Him.

And I remembered a Bible story so long ago, read to me by my grandmother about the Pharisee and the Publican, the one thanking God for not making him like other men, and the other, filled with humility, saying, "Oh, God, have mercy on me, a sinner."

What I really wanted was to make a deal with God . . . *quid pro quo* . . . I'll give You something, You give me something.

But what can you offer the Greatest Negotiator when you know that at this very instant, He can cause a heart to cease its ticking or cause an abused artery to blow out like a worn inner tube? But who abused it? God didn't. Who said the greatest gift God can give us was free will; our heart to abuse, our arteries and belly and bladder . . . our mind . . . our soul?

"Please God," I prayed, "give me back my health and a strong and affectionate heart; give me back my wife and kids; let them swing again and shout and laugh. And let me be around to hear it. I offer You my life for whatever remains of it. Do with me what You will . . . suffer the little children to come to me . . . oh, God, in the Name of your Son, Jesus, have mercy on me, a sinner. . . ."

I arose groggily, pushing against the bark of the tree, standing erect, conscious now of Duke John bounding up, huge paws pressing against my chest. As I stroked the noble head I was conscious too that the searing pain was gone from my head and rib cage. I breathed deeply, momentarily expecting a stab of pain, but nothing . . . pure, fresh, glorious air wafting into me, seeping down to my toes, giving me life, renewal.

Then I was suddenly aware of a gentle, quickening breeze through leaf-stripped boughs; strange, I thought, for this hour of the night . . . or morning. But I heard it above me as we trod the path back toward Chain Bridge, back toward home. The glittering moon was further on now, but still casting the shadows of trees across the trail. Stars still danced and winked above and below in the canal. We climbed the steep hill winding up to Arlington and there was the spire of Walker Chapel, stark white and bathed by twin flood lights. Above it, a cross, the ageless symbol. Only a symbol, Kevin had said so many years ago at a happy dinner table. Yes, a symbol, Bruce had agreed, but we have these symbols everywhere to remind us. True, Kevin had said, but it's what you really think that counts.

I entered the house stealthily, a house now dark and quiet and asleep, and I stole past Cella's door and paused to listen to the deep, untroubled sleep of my tennis champ unwinding. I went on to the guest room, and softly shut the door, turned on a bedside light and sat there on the edge of the bed browsing through an old and battered book of poetry, a gift from my loving mother, with poems mostly by Edgar A. Guest, her favorite, but others too.

As I skimmed through the book, I was stopped by a poem I seemed to have never read before—*If you but knew* it began. Somehow it seemed to sum up all I felt for Cella. After finishing it, I knew that later that day—for it was after midnight—that I would go alone to the old, rundown farm in central Virginia to think through what had happened to me. I set the alarm for six and scribbled a note to Cella and marked the poem for her in the book. I doused the light, crawled between the sheets and lay there in the dark, listening to the quiet house. But I was no longer alone and I remembered the poem's ending:

> Could you but learn
> How when you doubt my truth, I sadly yearn
> To tell you all, to stand for one brief space
> Unfettered, soul to soul, as face to face,
> To crown you queen, my queen, till life shall end,
> My one true love, my truest friend,
> Would you love me, dearest, as fondly in return,
> Could you but learn?

Chapter Eighteen

The Old Farmhouse

DUKE JOHN LAY BESIDE me, panting, tongue lolling out. Duke John was not a rabbit dog. He wasn't a bird dog either. He was a nothing dog, but beautiful and a good friend and faithful companion. He was a mostly snow-white Samoyed husky with a touch of cream about the shoulders. Duke's forebears were lead dogs on Alaskan sled teams, and, before that, caribou herders on the Samoyed Peninsula of Siberia.

The two of us were out hunting along Deep Run in central Virginia. It was late fall and the leaves were gone from the trees, clustering on the ground, multicolored. It was dry where we were lying, on a layer of oak leaves and pine needles with a warming November sun soaking through the wool plaid shirt, hot on my back. We were waiting there for another rabbit. Duke John was quiet, hind legs astraddle, front paws together, noble head raised and tongue lolling out. He whined a bit and I ran a gentle hand along that noble, worthless head, and then eased the safety off the little, single-shot, small-bore rifle.

I needed one more rabbit. We were out of meat and down to the last two-pound bag of Uncle Ben's converted rice. With the exception of Tuesday, Duke and I had subsisted on rabbit stew and rice. On that day, I bagged four quail with a little four-ten Ivor Johnson shotgun which is no mean feat even for a young and steady hand. But I had been off the sauce for nearly two months and some of the skills I thought were gone forever were slowly returning.

A cottontail hopped from the creek bed and sped through the stubble field. I steadied the rifle and drew a bead on him. *"Sprang,"* and the rabbit crumpled to the ground. Duke was up in an instant, barking excitedly and running to inspect the fallen animal. I jumped to my feet, grabbed a battered old fishing creel, heavy with three dead rabbits and ran to retrieve number four.

I dropped the cottontail into the creel, patted Great Hunter on the head and started the trek back to the old farmhouse—my home and Duke's now for five weeks. We had become accustomed to the place and looked forward to its snug, confining interior and evenings of hasenpfeffer. We trudged toward it, following the creek bed as it wound gently upward toward the high ground of the partially wooded, rolling prairie land. The tired, old barn with its caved-in roof and weatherbeaten board siding loomed on the horizon. Through the missing slats, I caught the red gleam of my son Kevin's Volkswagen which sat, unused, ever since that day I had driven up here five weeks before— a lifetime, really; or a transition from one life to another.

We passed the barn, Duke John racing after a squirrel which scampered up one of the tall oaks. I walked up the worn pathway leading to a rotting stoop and flipped the creel onto the sagging porch.

Easing open the creaking front door, I entered the dim interior of a combination kitchen and sitting room. A blackened, wood-burning cook stove dominated the far wall and near it, a wooden table with two high-backed, cane-bottomed chairs, the seat of one split and shredded. One chair was enough, for Duke John preferred a scruffy piece of carpet behind the stove.

A lone window stared from an adjacent wall, its panes layered with grime and rain-spattered dust. Beneath it sat an ancient davenport with cotton batting protruding. An unmatched barrel chair squatted nearby, and between them a three-legged table with a rusting cream can acting as a fourth. My electric typewriter rested there, and sheafs of unfinished manuscript next to a goose-neck lamp. An extension cord ran to a bare bulb in a double socket suspended by a threadbare cord from a cracked and peeling ceiling. A 1940 vintage Philco cabinet radio stood aloof in a far corner, once having a car battery as a source of power but silent for the past twenty years.

Home. Not the Watergate apartments, surely, but, for my needs of the moment, more than adequate.

The fire I banked that morning had died out and I busied myself tending a new one; kindling shaved with an old hunting knife and piled atop a few pages from a 1954 Montgomery Ward catalog; a few squirts of lighter fluid in true Boy Scout fashion, and soon, a flickering fire.

I drew a couple dippers of water from a ten-quart galvanized pail set next to the wood box, and partially filled a chipped enamel kettle which I placed over the open flame. Locating a whetstone, I took it and the hunting knife to the front porch and sat next to the creel where I honed an edge on the blade in preparation for rabbit skinning. Duke, bored with an elusive squirrel, pranced over and rested his head on my knee.

I skinned one of the rabbits and by that time, the kettle was singing and I went in and browsed in the nearly bare larder for the last of the tea bags. There was a half-gallon bottle of Johnnie Walker Red Label Scotch next to the Lipton's carton. I took down the bottle and removed the cork, recalling Goldie Flynn's eternal query, "Three glooks do it?"

I poured a bit into a tumbler and added a quarter dipper of water from the pail, shook it gently and sniffed the contents: the sweet, burnt odor of good Scotch. I walked to the rear door, tugged it open and cast the drink to the wind. Ceremony over, I recorked the bottle and slid it back on the dusty shelf, then plucked out the one remaining tea bag from the carton. How refreshing—a cup of hot tea!

I cut a slice of homemade sourdough bread. I had been baking once a week using stone ground whole wheat flour and batter which I kept in a crock atop the warming ovens of the stove. Occasionally, the crock would bubble over and fill the room with a pungent, yeasty smell.

In the corner of the kitchen, near a crude brick fireplace, was a cupboard with unfinished pine boards serving as shelves. On them were four books: my library. Strange books for an arms peddler: Fulton Sheehan's *Peace of Soul,* Fulton Oursler's *Why I Know There Is a God,* Merton's *The Seven Storey Mountain* and Catherine Marshall's *A Man Called Peter.* I selected the latter for the evening ritual of reading, to go with the whole wheat bread and tepid tea. It was a raggedy, once-brown volume with frayed corners and dog-eared pages; it was a well-read book but not by me, the eternal skeptic more used to reading *Interavia.*

As I flipped through the pages of *A Man Called Peter,* my mind went back to a miserably cold night in Korea in 1953. I had taken out a combat patrol at sunset through the Chor'won Valley. We got into a fire fight at midnight against a stronger force of Chinese. Early in the fog-shrouded morning, we disengaged and staggered back to the main line of resistance. I carried a wounded boy doped with morphine. Back in the aid tent the boy from Montana, looking pasty faced and haggard, clutched my hand with a fierce grip, tears on his cheeks. "I don't wanna die, Lieutenant."

But he died there on the table with the two kerosene lanterns casting flickering shadows on the murky walls of the tent.

And now Peter Marshall was challenging his flock: "I came not to invite the pious but the irreligious." And ". . . He needs red-blooded men and women now . . . Vigorous they are. They like life." And later, "Some of you have drifted long enough."

The words were strong tonight, and each hit like an arrow's shaft. ". . . He will give you what it takes." I set the book down.

As I sat there at the rickety table with the one dim bulb burning, I closed my eyes and clasped my hands together and remembered the words of Sean O'Malley the last time I saw him in front of our house in Arlington. "Remember, Donn, that He told us two thousand years ago and He keeps remindin' us: 'Ask anything in my name and it shall be yours.' Don't be ashamed to ask."

I sat there for awhile remembering O'Malley and Flynn and Maria Valdez and Billie Mason and our hectic times together. And my wife, Ursella, and our six kids—the good times, the trials, the travail. I thought of the boys and their problems. Kevin had gone on to Fort Knox and become a tanker; and after that, to Germany to an armored unit with the First Division. He had become an outstanding soldier. I was proud of all my children. Now, I wished I had let them know it earlier.

"Hey, Lord," I prayed. "I'm pretty new at this, but I need Your help . . . Your guidance. Things have pretty much come apart at the seams, and I can't hold them together much longer by myself. I need your understanding and some fortitude and strength. And humility too . . . and patience . . . I ask this in the name of your Son, Jesus." I mumbled, searching for a fitting ending to my unaccustomed plea for assistance.

So easy to stray from the path, I thought; so difficult to find it again. I ate the last morsel of bread and washed it down with the dregs of the tea. Rising from the table, I finished cleaning the rabbits and dropped them into a pail half filled with water and a handful of salt. I set them inside and went out the rear door and beyond the outhouse where I had felled two massive, dead, oak trees the day before. Each day, I spent at least two hours either dropping trees or chopping them into sections approximately fifteen inches in length, and splitting the sections into stove-sized pieces. It not only served as fuel for warmth and cooking but was vigorous exercise and therapeutic as well. I needed both.

The sun was slipping behind the Blue Ridge skyline as I carried an armful of split slabs into the kitchen and dumped them into the woodbox. I jerked the chain on the light bulb fixture and set to cutting up the rabbits, rolling each piece in a mixture of flour, salt, and pepper.

As I greased the iron fry pan, I heard Duke's excited barking. Then I heard the car drive up. I walked out to the porch as she opened the car door and slid out, skirt riding up. I remembered also the swivel-hipped stride of an athlete, used to tennis courts and swimming pools and horses.

"Donn . . . Donn . . ." she said.

I grinned at her, choking back the tears. What an amazing wife I had—patient, courageous, skillful, resourceful, understanding!

"Aren't you going to invite me in, Darling?"

"Why yes," I said. "Yes, come in. We're having hassenpfeffer."

And later that evening, we saddled the two horses and rode into the high pasture. The night turned chilly and it was clear with a million or so stars. We rode up to the crest of the hill in silence, the only sound the creaking of saddle leather and the occasional snort of a horse. We reined in at the top near two entwined hickory trees which Cella named the Wedding Tree, each of them imperfect; and yet, together, a perfect tree.

"Welcome home, Daddy," she said, and I reached for her hand. "You're going to do great things out here."

"Correction," I said. "We. *We're* going to do great things out here . . . the three of us . . ."

I think she understood.

Epilogue

OCTOBER OF 1978: another gorgeous fall in Virginia with the Blue Ridge Mountains standing tall and clear against the azure. The gently rolling fields and meadows of the Grand Pre farm, lush and verdant from ample rain, stretch to the distant woods, now a breathtaking rainbow hue of red and yellow and green and brown and orange. We are farmers now, raising corn and cattle and quarter horses.

And kids. As one local reporter described it: Grand Pre Farm is "the quietest school in Virginia. It is quiet because none of the pupils either hears or speaks. None of them can really see either. Mark is totally sightless. Jimmy, Chris, Teresa, Nesa and Tad all can see a little but are legally blind."

Cella had worked with deaf-blind children for years. We have taken her knowledge and a select group of other dedicated and knowledgeable people and established The National Association for Deaf-Blind Children. It is a tax-exempt, charitable organization, relying almost entirely on volunteers. The paid staff are special educators and health care personnel. Our board of directors is composed of unpaid professionals: ministers, medical doctors, businessmen and housewives whose "payment" comes in the form of intrinsic pleasure; watching multihandicapped children grow and learn and adjust to their environment.

It was Goldie Flynn and Father O'Malley who had earlier urged us to set up a center for not only deaf-blind children but any child with more than one handicap. We started the center, not with Flynn's money, but with O'Malley's prayers and our own and those of our

197

friends; and now, we know that prayer can move mountains, since a veritable mountain of forms and paperwork and bureaucratic requirements had stood in our way of becoming established and licensed as a child care facility and a private school. But we discovered something else: even in the faceless and anonymous bureaucracy, there are people; and as you deal with them, they become personalities; and as they saw what we were attempting, a few helped us, if not to move the mountain, to surmount it anyway. We now have our necessary licenses and certificates and are receiving our first children.

We have built our first facility—literally built it ourselves here on the farm. We will build other homes, for the whole concept of our center is built around the home—the family. Within each home, there are parents. Some have their natural children, all have up to ten multi-handicapped children, living together, working together, loving together. Our handicapped children are boys and girls between the ages of six and fourteen who, within the structure of the home, learn the daily living skills, and within the schoolrooms learn to communicate, to read and write and do arithmetic; learn to work together and to play together.

Another aspect of our center is the work with student teachers and social workers. They come here to do practice teaching from Gallaudet College in Washington, from George Mason College in Fairfax County, from James Madison University in Harrisonburg, from the University of Virginia in Charlottesville.

Our third facet is working with parents of handicapped children. Whether their children are here at the center or are at home or enrolled in the public schools, we offer workshops for the parents, to help them cope with the problems in raising a multihandicapped child.

We have great plans for the future: Louise Ward Elliott, wife of Professor William Yandell Elliott, former head of the Harvard University Department of Government and advisor to Presidents, has offered her Hidden Valley Farm of one thousand acres to us so we can expand into a vocational school for older handicapped youths; a place where they can learn meaningful skills and do meaningful work for private industrial firms in sheltered workshops.

Regardless of what we do in the future, we will stick to the family concept: small groups of children working and playing and learning together under the guidance of house parents.

For it was this engrained family concept that brought me back to reality. It was my family who built our present seven-bedroom, four-bath home which is now headquarters for Grand Pre Farm in Madison County. It was Bruce, a graduate of George Washington University and his lovely wife, Karen Dewberry, who did the design work and interior decorating; Doneva's husband, Dale, a master builder, guided us, board by board and brick by brick. Doneva is director of recreation for the handicapped children. Kevin and Colin pounded nails and sawed lumber and carried mortar on weekends; Kevin who drives an eighteen-wheeler and is "Smokestack" to his good CB buddies; Colin, in his second year at Northern Virginia College who bags groceries at Safeway in the evenings to cover his living expenses in Arlington; and Annette, who at 17 is a lovely, vivacious blonde, recently graduated from Yorktown High School. She and her girl friend, Lisa McLaughlin, another blonde equally as lovely and vivacious, are giving us a year of their lives at the center before they enter college next fall. They are serving as teaching assistants and counselors; they are painting interior and exterior trim on the new home, placing insulating batts in the crawl space, training four yearling quarter horses to drive and ride, and even hauling hay bales and operating the big Massey Ferguson tractor with the bush hog on the rear.

And, of course, there is Thaddeus Daniel—the Tadpole—who is an energetic 11 and who, despite severe loss of hearing and sight, is exceptionally intelligent and able to read and write, add and subtract. He may never become a college professor or a medical doctor or a lawyer, but he will have a good life and a full one. He and his classmates are lucky in that here at the farm they have a home and opportunity, although deep down we know we are lucky to have them. For they give us all an undefinable appreciation of how the game of life can be played with two strikes already called.

One of Kevin's girl friends summed it up a few years ago as she sat with Tad on her lap in front of the fireplace in our Arlington home:

"You hold out your hand to help the Tadpole, but he ends up showing you what it's all about. He knows that the sun is warm and the snow is soft and the rain is wet; and that it's fun to run and great to be tossed up high; and that baking cookies smell good and taste better; and that when you're not really sure of where you're going, it's comforting to reach out and find the hand of a friend. The Tadpole teaches us to love each other and trust in God, our heavenly Father."

Isn't that what it's all about?

Author's Note

CHRISTMAS 1978 APPROACHES. It has been two years since I first met the people at Chosen Books; two years since Jean Brown read my letter to Len LeSourd and thereby "discovered" me; two years of working closely with the many members of the Chosen Books staff, more like a big family than a business.

There was Len LeSourd shepherding me through several rewrites, excising whole chapters from the text, dropping Saudi Arabia and Ethiopia and Iran and Morocco and Kuwait: "You can use these in another book."

And Tib Sherrill encouraging me: "You have 'born' qualities that no amount of teaching can give a writer, but you lack control. Don't worry," she added, "we can teach you control."

They did. Catherine Marshall telling me that I could write and encouraging me to write and telling me to tighten up the story; her mother, Mrs. Wood—"Christy" of one of Catherine's novels—encouraging me to write.

There were Dick and Betty Schneider who became like brother and sister to Ursella and me as we shaped a new life on our farm in Madison County. They would visit us there and we would work on the book in particular and life in general.

It was Dick, who along with Gordon Carlson, blue penciled—and red penciled—my "final" manuscript two or three times; and Stacey Walde who typed the manuscript just as many times.

So, two years have come and gone and another Christmas approaches, and as I dwell on its true meaning, I think back to certain questions John F. Kennedy asked back in 1960 when he ran for the presidency:

"Can a nation organized and governed such as ours endure? That is the real question. Have we the nerve and the will? Can we carry through in an age where we will witness not only new breakthroughs in weapons of destruction but also a race for mastery of the sky and the rain, the ocean and the tides, the far side of space and the inside of men's minds?"

The answer for me is simple, maybe even simplistic in this age of enlightenment: Yes, if we return to the teachings of Christ. This, to me, is the "candle" of which Kennedy spoke when he said, again in 1960: "We are not here to curse the darkness but to light the candle that can guide us through that darkness to a safe and sane future . . . "